INCREDIBLE
OLYMPIC
FEATS

AMONG OTHER BOOKS BY JIM BENAGH

Incredible Athletic Feats (1969)
Incredible Football Feats (1974)
Incredible Basketball Feats (1974)
Incredible Baseball Feats (1975)

INCREDIBLE OLYMPIC FEATS

Jim Benagh

McGraw-Hill Book Company

New York St. Louis San Francisco London Paris Düsseldorf
Tokyo Kuala Lumpur Mexico Montreal Panama São Paulo
Sydney Toronto Johannesburg New Delhi Singapore

Book design by Stan Drate.

Copyright © 1976 by Jim Benagh. All rights reserved. Printed in the United States of America. No part of this publication may be reproduced, stored in a retrieval system, or transmitted, in any form or by any means, electronic, mechanical, photocopying, recording, or otherwise, without the prior written permission of the publisher.

First McGraw-Hill Book Company Edition, 1976
1 2 3 4 5 6 7 8 9 M U M U 7 9 8 7 6

Library of Congress Cataloging in Publication Data
Benagh, Jim, 1937–
   Incredible Olympic feats.

    1. Olympic games—History. I. Title.
GV721.5.B375   796.4'8   75-33237
ISBN 0-07-004426-0

CONTENTS

FOREWORD — xi

1896 OLYMPICS
The First U.S. Team Came, Saw, and Conquered — 1

1900 ROWING
A Mystery Boy Gets the Netherlands out of Dutch — 5

1900 TRACK AND FIELD
Three American Roommates = 14 Olympic Medals — 8

1900–1908 TRACK AND FIELD
Ray Ewry Was a Standup Guy—and a 10-Gold Winner — 10

1904 TRACK AND FIELD
Archie Hahn Scored a Triple Victory in the Sprints — 12

1908 TRACK AND FIELD
Wyndham Halswelle Ran Alone to Get His Medal — 14

1908–1948 FENCING
Ivan Osiier Competed for Four Decades   17

1912 SOCCER
G. E. Fuchs Scored Ten Goals in a Game   18

1912 TRACK AND FIELD, 1948 YACHTING
Ralph Craig's Olympic Comeback Took 36 Years   19

1920–1936 ICE HOCKEY
Canada Ruled the World in Flawless Fashion   21

1920 SHOOTING
Oscar Swahn Won a Medal at Age 73   24

1920 BOXING, 1932 BOBSLED
Eddie Eagan's Second Gold Was Tougher than His First   26

1924 ICE HOCKEY
Harry Watson Went beyond the "Hat Trick"   28

1924 TRACK AND FIELD
Paavo Nurmi–Willie Ritola Rivalry Helped the Finns   29

1924 TRACK AND FIELD
Bob Le Gendre Was a Jump Ahead of the Olympics   32

1924 SWIMMING AND DIVING
Aileen Riggin Achieved a Unique Aquatic Double   35

1924–1936 FIGURE SKATING
Sonja Henie Went from Last to First   37

1932–1960 FENCING
Aladar Gerevich Was Sharp for Six Olympics   39

1936 TRACK AND FIELD
Jesse Owens's Records Were Made to Last   40

1936 TRACK AND FIELD
The "Black Auxiliaries" Chased Hitler out of His Stadium   45

1936 TRACK AND FIELD
Hermann Ratjin Almost Pulled an Upset for *Der Fuehrer*   48

1936 DIVING
Marjorie Gestring Took Her Doll to the Games and Took a Medal Home   50

1936 SHOOTING
Willy Rogeberg Was a Shooting Star   52

1936–1972 BASKETBALL
The Americans Were Good at Their Own Game   53

1948 TRACK AND FIELD
Bob Mathias Was the "Boy Wonder" of All Time   61

1948 TRACK AND FIELD
Harrison Dillard Overcame a Hurdle   65

1948–1960 YACHTING
Paul Elvstrom Went from Novice to Master 70

1948–1964 WATER POLO, 1952–1972 SWIMMING
The Gyarmatis Made the Olympics a Family Affair 73

1948–1956 BOXING
Laszlo Papp Didn't Beat around the Bushes 75

1952 FIGURE SKATING
Dick Button Executed a Triple Loop Jump 77

1952 TRACK AND FIELD
The Jamaicans Won a Relay Fair and Square 80

1952 TRACK AND FIELD
Emil Zatopek's Triple Was Nearly Miraculous 84

1952 BOXING
Floyd Patterson, at 17, Made a Step toward Fame 87

1952–1956 DIVING
Pat McCormick Won a Double Double 89

1956 TRACK AND FIELD
Hellsten and Ignatyev Went to the Wire for a Medal 91

1956–1968 TRACK AND FIELD
Al Oerter Was Unbeatable in the Clutch 93

1956–1964 SWIMMING
Dawn Fraser Got Better As She Got Older — 98

1956–1964 GYMNASTICS
Larisa Latynina Won a Record Number of Medals — 100

1960 ICE HOCKEY
The Americans Benefited from Some Russian Detente — 102

1960 BASKETBALL
Jerry Lucas Had a Perfect Game — 105

1960 SWIMMING
Jeff Farrell's Guts Made Up for His Appendix — 107

1960 TRACK AND FIELD
Otis Davis Came out of Nowhere to Win the 400 — 110

1960–1964 TRACK AND FIELD
Abebe Bikila's "Footwork" Won Him Marathon Titles — 114

1964 SPEED SKATING
Lidija Skoblikova Was a Paavo Nurmi on Ice — 118

1964 SKIING
The Goitschel Sisters Go 1–2 . . . and 2–1 — 121

1964 TRACK AND FIELD
Billy Mills Shocked Everybody but Himself — 124

1964 VOLLEYBALL
Japan's Women Treated Defeat Like Death   **126**

1968 TRACK AND FIELD
Bob Beamon Jumped for Joy High above Sea Level   **128**

1972 GYMNASTICS
Olga Korbut Bent over Backward for Her Fans   **131**

1972 WRESTLING
Ivan Yarygin Pinned Defeat on Opponents   **135**

1972 TRACK AND FIELD
Kip Keino's Form Was Strictly Championship   **137**

1972 TRACK AND FIELD
Lasse Viren "Rose" to the Occasion   **139**

1972 SWIMMING
Mark Spitz Was the Greatest Goldfish of Them All   **142**

1972 SWIMMING
Shane Gould Logged Her Share of Time in the Water, Too   **145**

GOLD MEDAL WINNERS/SUMMER OLYMPICS 1896–1972   **147**

GOLD MEDAL WINNERS/WINTER OLYMPICS 1924–1972   **174**

FOREWORD

The Olympic Games hold a unique position in the world of sports. For one thing, the Olympics are truly international in scope, unlike many big-time sports which are identified with a single nation, a group of countries, or a geographical area. For another thing, the kaleidoscope of Olympic activities—with so many varied events—makes for a wide range of interest and enjoyment to everyone, sports fan or not.

But more important, the Olympics are staged every four years. This heightens the drama. The athlete must sharpen his or her skills for that long period of time, and keep them sharp if the goal is a coveted Olympic medal. Four years is a long time to build up interest in a competition, too, and this anticipation adds to the drama.

At the end of the four-year wait, there is that moment when a lesser athlete can pull an upset and become better known round the world than a world record holder. Or, by the same logic, the build-up, the suspense, can psyche and push a world record holder to even greater feats. The fact that the Olympics are staged every four years also means, in many cases, that this is the only time all the great athletes in the respective events are assembled; this too raises the level of competition and therefore affects the level of the final results.

In such an aura of competition are not only the record-setting performances but also the other phases of sports drama: young against old; old against time; large against small, whether it be persons or nations; comebacks; upsets; dynasties; versatility; teamwork; and so on.

The purpose of *Incredible Olympic Feats* is to relate some of that drama. Many of the names in the book are familiar ones, but *Incredible Olympic Feats* tries to go beyond the basic facts in retelling the accomplishments. It is hoped that *Incredible Olympic Feats* will introduce the reader to feats not generally known. In many cases, there are no specific Olympic records kept on the topics chosen for this book.

The topics were chosen for variety's sake—from many different sports in both the Summer and Winter Olympics. There should be something for everyone.

The author wishes to thank the many athletes, sportswriters, fans, and others who have over the years contributed material that made this book possible. I am especially grateful to the International Olympic Committee in Switzerland; the United States Olympic Committee in New York City (and particularly to C. Robert Paul); the hosts at the three Olympic Games I attended (Rome, Mexico City, and Munich); Jesse Abramson; Bill Bowerman; Jim Dunaway; M. H. Reid of the Hockey Hall of Fame in Toronto, Canada; the staffs of the New York City and Englewood, New Jersey, public libraries; *Track & Field News*; and Hiag Akmakjian, who helped to develop the book from its inception.

The author would be grateful to hear from Olympic fans who may have feats to add to further editions of the book. The address is Post Office Box 1113, Englewood Cliffs, New Jersey 07632, U.S.A.

JIM BENAGH

1896 OLYMPICS
The First U.S. Team Came, Saw, and Conquered

When the 15 members of the United States contingent arrived in Athens for the revival of the Olympic Games in 1896, they looked, as the saying goes, as if they had just got off the boat. Indeed they had. Traveling by tramp steamer across the Atlantic, the Americans had come farther than any of the other athletes of 12 nations who would partake in the revival of the ancient rites of Greece.

And no team seemed to spell out better the amateur ideals conceived by Baron de Coubertin, founder of the modern Olympics, than the U.S. squad. The 14 athletes plus a track trainer had ventured to Athens on their own. There was no U.S. Olympic Committee nor a massive fund-raising machine behind them. A few of the track and field athletes had support from the Boston Athletic Association, but for the most part the Americans paid their own way. The trip by tramp steamer left the 11 track and field athletes with heavy sea legs, and the lone swimmer had lots of water to look at but none to train in. The other participants, two brothers scheduled for pistol-shooting events, did not have to be concerned with staying in shape.

The Greeks, enthusiastic and delighted over the revival of the Games, proved to be good hosts—almost too good. They burdened the Americans with lengthy speeches, marched them around the city over and over again, then almost drowned them with endless toasts of white wine. The Americans had to compete the next day.

The Greeks, who had been the first civilized nation to elevate the role of sports so many centuries before, liked having the upstart Americans in their Games. But at least one hotelkeeper where they were staying let them know that not only were the Greeks the first to start sports, they were going to be the first in the 1896 Games too. The hotelkeeper told Thomas Curtis, after a burst of laughter when he found out the American was a hurdler, that he had come a long 5,000 miles to finish second. The Greeks, he said, had an excellent hurdler who was at his peak.

But the Americans had made a big sacrifice to get to Athens, so there would be no turning back on the eve of the Games.

The next day, U.S. trackmen swept all three heats of the 100 meters to open the competition after a 15-century lapse. One of the heat winners was Thomas Curtis. And the first Olympic winner in over 1,500 years turned out to be triple-jumper James Connolly, who gave up his college education at Harvard to go to Athens when his dean denied him a leave of absence. Connolly's best leap was just shy of 45 feet, modest by current standards but an easy victory then.

The Greeks were more interested in the discus throw, however. After all, here was a truly national event, conceived in the country itself and bearing a Greek name. A local hero, Panagiotis Paraskevopoulos, was supposed to be able to whirl the discus distances that were in keeping with the length of his name. The Greeks had other entrants in the event too who knew their way around the discus circle.

The American candidate in the competition had a distinct disadvantage. Robert Garrett, a Princeton student, had been practicing with a makeshift discus back in the United States and had never picked up a real one until he got to Athens. Fortunately, a friendly Greek presented him with one to use at the meet.

Paraskevopoulos got the lead and maintained it for most of the match. His teammate kept a hold on second place. Then on his final throw, with the favored Greek leading with a 95-foot toss, Garrett spun the discus 95 feet $7^{3}/_{4}$ inches to win. It was the first major upset in modern Olympic history, and considering that Garrett had never touched a real discus before that day, it had to be one of the greatest upsets of any Olympics, past or present.

One by one, the Americans began piling up gold, silver, and bronze medals, much to the surprise of their Greek hosts and the other European stars. In shooting, the two Paine brothers (John and Sumner) each won a revolver event. In the hurdles, Curtis beat his "unbeatable" Greek foe.

Only in swimming did the Americans have a letdown. Their only entry, Gardner Williams, was a bit shocked to learn that his events would be held in a cold bay off the Mediterranean Sea instead of in the comfort of a pool. Nevertheless, he took a fourth and fifth place.

In all, the Americans won 9 of 12 track and field events. That, coupled with the shooting medals, gave them a total of 11 gold medals, more than any other team.

It was a nice way to start an Olympics—and it would set a precedent for American teams in years to come.

The U.S. contingent had one more task to do before bringing their gold back to their country, though. Having taught their hosts something about the ancient Greek sports, the Americans decided to teach them something about an American sport too. The U.S. team cut into their hosts' post-Olympic celebration to have a game of baseball. One of the participants they enticed into play was the King of Greece himself.

THE FIRST U.S. OLYMPIC TEAM

Track and Field

Arthur Blake	1,500 meters	2d place
Thomas Burke	100 meters	1st place
	400 meters	1st place
Ellery Clark	Long jump	1st place
	High jump	1st place
James Connolly	Triple jump	1st place
	High jump	2d place
	Long jump	3d place
Thomas Curtis	110-meter hurdles	1st place
	100 meters	4th place
Robert Edgren	Shot put, discus	Did not place
Robert Garrett	Shot put	1st place
	Discus	1st place
	Long jump	2d place
	High jump	3d place
William Hoyt	Pole vault	1st place
	110-meter hurdles	Did not place
Herbert Jamison	400 meters	2d place
Francis Lane	100 meters	5th place
Alfred Tyler	Pole vault	2d place

Shooting

John Paine	Military revolver	1st place
	Choice revolver	Did not place
Sumner Paine	Military revolver	2d place
	Choice revolver	1st place

Swimming

Gardner Williams	100-meter freestyle	5th place
	1,500-meter freestyle	4th place

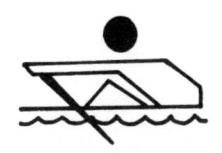

1900 ROWING
A Mystery Boy Got the Netherlands out of Dutch

The 1900 Olympics, held in Paris, were in trouble from beginning to end—and part of the problem was that the beginning was too far from the end. After the Greeks hosted such a tremendous revival of the Games in 1896, interest mounted in other countries to stage the contests in the next Olympiad, 1900. A lot of people felt that the Games should maintain a permanent home in Greece: after all, no country was so identified with the Olympic movement. But Baron de Coubertin, who was instrumental and influential in the revival, held that the Games should be circulated to major countries around the world. So he chose France for the second modern Games.

Unfortunately, the Paris Games were too closely linked to the international exposition (World's Fair) being held in the historic city at the same time. The Games were treated as a part of the exposition, and thus suffered greatly by being overshadowed. In fact, the exposition leaders even avoided the word "Olympics" whenever possible and preferred to call the Games "international championships." They were drawn out to coincide with the summer-long exposition too. Facilities and organization were the poorest of any Olympics, past or future. Would-be fans were apathetic, to say the least.

Still, 16 nations sent 1,505 athletes to compete over the five-month span. Or was it 1,506 athletes?

In this setting of confusion, one of the biggest mysteries in the history of the Olympics emerged.

Rowing was added to the 1900 Olympic agenda. Sculling was a popular sport around the world at the time—and in fact was a big betting sport in many of the English-speaking countries. The Greeks had put on a rowing exhibition in 1896, but there was no competition. The French, with powerful rowers and good facilities, made certain there would be some events in Paris.

One of those events was the coxed pairs, sometimes called "pairs with coxswain." The French had a couple of good teams entered, including their strong Societé de la Marne tandem. The French chances seemed quite good, particularly after a doctor who coxed the Netherlands team weighed in too heavy after the heats. At the last moment, though, the Dutch team showed up for the final with a new coxswain.

Nobody knew his name. Or his age. But somehow the Dutch rowers had enlisted a young boy, believed to be French. Those who recalled the scene said he couldn't have been more than 10 years old and probably was much less than that.

But there was no protest, probably because the smug French men figured they had the race sewed up after seeing the little boy at the stern of the Amsterdam-based Dutch craft. The little guy did okay, though. The race was close from start to finish and the Netherlands tandem won the sprint to the finish line—with a time of 7:34.2 to 7:34.4

minutes over Société de la Marne. Nobody knows what happened to the boy after the race, or even if he got a gold medal. But he had to be the youngest Olympic winner ever—judging by the comments of those who had a fleeting glance at his boyish face.

1900 TRACK AND FIELD
Three American Roommates = 14 Olympic Medals

At least three Americans at the second modern Olympics at Paris in 1900 were certain they would have somebody cheering for them. How did they know? Because before they left for Paris, the trio had been roommates and close friends in college.

The threesome consisted of Alvin Kraenzlein, Irving Baxter, and J. Walter Tewksbury. In Philadelphia the year before the Olympics, the three shared an apartment while they attended the University of Pennsylvania. All were versatile track stars, so when the call went out for a U.S. team to go to Paris, the three answered it.

At the 1900 Games, Kraenzlein was the first to win on the opening day. He won the 110-meter hurdles. His roommates cheered him on. But after that, there was little time to watch each other because all three athletes had full schedules.

Baxter and Tewksbury had five events each on their

slates. The springy Baxter hopped around the infield, taking the high jump and the pole vault to become the only Olympian ever to complete that rare double. Then he finished second in all three of the standing jumps behind American teammate Ray Ewry. Tewksbury won the 400-meter hurdles, an event not even contested in the United States. He also won a gold medal in the 200-meter dash. In his other running events, he collected two silver medals and a bronze.

What Kraenzlein didn't match in quantity with his roommates, he made up for in quality.

The Wisconsin native was entered in "only" four events—the 60-meter dash, the 110- and 200-meter hurdles, and the long jump. Kraenzlein won them all, beating Tewksbury twice in the process. He thus became the only Olympian to win four individual events in track and field.

But there was no need for jealousy. Among the three, they won eight gold medals, five silvers, and a bronze. That was more medals than any other nation earned in all track and field events in 1900.

1900–1908 TRACK AND FIELD
Ray Ewry Was a Standup Guy— and a 10-Gold Winner

One of the most remarkable performances in Olympic history won't ever be repeated unless they change the rules. But then again, the Olympics may never see another performer like Ray Ewry.

A former polio victim who took up sports to rebuild his weak legs, Ewry tried track and field at Purdue University after a football injury sidelined him from that sport. That was in the 1890s.

By the time the second Olympics were held in 1900, Ewry was already 26, which signals the downward trend of many American track stars' careers. But Ewry was only beginning. That year he won three gold medals on one day alone (July 16) at Paris. His specialties were the standing jumps (standing high jump, standing long jump, standing triple jump), which have since been discontinued. Ewry, who stood 6 feet 3 inches, was so dominant at Paris that he jumped nearly a half foot higher than the best competition in the high jump.

In the 1904 Olympics, Ewry again won three golds in the same events.

In the special 1906 Olympics—the only one held in an off-year—the standing triple jump (or hop, step, and jump, as it was often called then) was eliminated. But Ewry was still the best man around in the standing long jump and high jump. He won again.

In 1908, when he was 34 years old, Ewry wrapped up his Olympic career with victories in the standing long and high jumps again. His gold medal total was now at ten—a count that has never been surpassed in track, where the next best individual total is seven. The standing jumps were eliminated from the Olympics after 1912. Ewry competed until he was 38.

RAY EWRY'S OLYMPIC VICTORIES

Event	Result	Comment
1900		
Standing high jump	1st, 5' 5"	Olympic record; 5' 8⁷/₈" was third in *running* high jump that year
Standing long jump	1st, 10' 6.4"	Olympic record
Standing triple jump	1st, 34' 8¹/₂"	Olympic record
1904		
Standing high jump	4' 11"	
Standing long jump	11' 4⁷/₈"	World record which stood until 1938, when event was discarded
Standing triple jump	1st, 34' 7¹/₄"	
1906		
Standing high jump	1st, 5' 1⁵/₈"	
Standing long jump	1st, 10' 10"	
1908		
Standing high jump	1st, 5' 2"	
Standing long jump	1st, 10' 11¹/₄"	

1904 TRACK AND FIELD
Archie Hahn Scored a Triple Victory in the Sprints

Winning two short sprint events in the Olympics is no easy task, but seven men have done it through the 1972 Games. The last six were Ralph Craig of the United States, 1912; Percy Williams of Canada, 1928; Eddie Tolan of the United States, 1932; Jesse Owens of the United States, 1936; Bobby Morrow of the United States, 1956; and Valery Borzov of the Soviet Union, 1972.

The first man to do it managed to one-up his successors by winning not just two but three sprints.

Archie Hahn, a star from the University of Michigan running for the United States at St. Louis in 1904, not only set Olympic records in the 100 and 200, but also won the 60-meter dash in 7 seconds flat. Hahn had an edge on his successors, though, because the 60 was dropped after the 1904 Games.

But he was no slouch on the track. His 21.6-second clocking in the 200 wasn't broken until 1928 (Hahn had an edge there, too, because he ran on a straightaway), and he won the 100 again at the unofficial Olympics at Athens in 1906.

If Hahn's triple was unusual, so were some others during the 1904 Games.

Consider what some of Hahn's American teammates did:

Ray Ewry got three golds for his standing jumps (see page 11).

Jim Lightbody won an odd triple in the 800 meters, 1,500 meters, and 2,500-meter steeplechase.

Harry Hillman was first across the line in the 200-meter hurdles, 400-meter hurdles, and 400-meter run.

Like Hahn, all would prove themselves winners again in future Olympics. And like Hahn's, their feats can't be matched unless the Olympic track and field format is changed.

Ewry's standing jumps have been eliminated, Lightbody's 2,500-meter steeplechase has been lengthened to 3,000 meters, and Hillman's 200-meter hurdle event has long since been dropped.

1908 TRACK AND FIELD
Wyndham Halswelle Ran Alone to Get His Medal

The 1908 Olympics had all the makings of another Revolutionary War between the United States and Great Britain, this time to be battled on English soil—or cinders. The Games were in London that year, and they were plagued with controversies, often pitting the Americans against the British in matters of rules decisions and interpretations. No matter who was at fault, nothing matched the final race of the 400-meter dash for bitterness.

The Americans were loaded with 400-meter men and won seven of nine places for the semifinals. Three Americans—J. B. Taylor, J. C. Carpenter, and W. C. Robbins—made it to the four-man final along with Lt. Wyndham Halswelle of Great Britain.

Halswelle was a splendid runner who raced his first 400 in 49.4 seconds, just shy of the Olympic mark at the time. Then he sped through the semifinals in 48.4 to smash the

Games record. But the Americans were no slouches, either, and it figured to be anyone's race for the scheduled Thursday, July 23, final.

Taylor pretty much lost his chance when he was slow out of the start. The former University of Pennsylvania runner had won his semifinal heat in 49.8, fastest of the Americans.

Robbins, Carpenter, and Halswelle shot out in front, with Robbins soon taking the pole position and Carpenter in close pursuit. Halswelle was right up with the American pair, though. It was a wide-open race going into the last 100 meters.

As Robbins led the field, Carpenter pulled out in an effort to go around him on the turn. As he did, Halswelle was coming up fast, too, and Carpenter made accidental contact with him. The judges screamed foul.

Then, in a flurry, an official ruled the race void. The finish-line tape was cut before Carpenter arrived there. Taylor, way back and trying to catch up, was jerked off the track by another official.

The stands were quiet as an announcer gave a brief and unclear message over a megaphone that the race was void. He didn't say why.

A decision was made to rerun the race two days later, on Saturday when the Games would come to a close. The U.S. officials, who included Amos Alonzo Stagg (the famous football coach) and James Sullivan (whose name is on the Sullivan Award for outstanding American amateur athletes), disagreed violently. They maintained, as did the runners, that Halswelle could have passed Carpenter on either side. They added that while Carpenter was on the pole, he had left room on the inside for Halswelle to go by. Furthermore, they said, Halswelle didn't have the steam left to beat them, and that's why the British officials were acting the way they were. But the disclaimers were all in vain. The race was set for noon Saturday, and the 1908 Olympic 400 champion would be crowned then.

The Sullivan committee ordered the Americans not to run.

So, come Saturday, Halswelle had the track all to himself. He could have walked around and gotten a gold medal. But he chose to run to the best of his ability. He was clocked at 50 seconds flat, which was not bad in the loneliness of a short-distance runner.

1908–1948 FENCING
Ivan Osiier Competed for Four Decades

Fencing is a sport that man or woman can compete in for longer periods than more strenuous activities. But a Danish fencer one-upped his fellow swashbuckling competitors.

Ivan Osiier took part in his first Olympics in 1908. He took part in his last one in 1948, some four decades later.

In those four decades, Osiier went to seven Olympics. He purposely missed the 1936 Games as a protest against Adolf Hitler's use of the Games as propaganda. Had there not been two World Wars, Osiier might have competed in an incredible total of 11 Olympics.

And what did he have to show for all those trips?

In 1912, Osiier was a close runner-up for the gold medal in the individual épée competition.

1912 SOCCER
G. E. Fuchs Scored Ten Goals in a Game

The German soccer team didn't make it to the final rounds of the 1912 Olympics. But that didn't stop the team's star center-forward from doing his best in a consolation round game with Russia.

On July 1, G. E. Fuchs scored a record ten goals, the best ever by an Olympian.

They were spread over the two halves of a not so exciting 16–0 game.

1912 TRACK AND FIELD, 1948 YACHTING
Ralph Craig's Olympic Comeback Took 36 Years

During his lifetime, Ralph Craig participated in 20 amateur sports, many at a high competitive level. A native of Detroit, Michigan, and a standout track star at the University of Michigan, Craig culminated his sports career at a fairly young age when he sprinted for the U.S. Olympic team at Stockholm in 1912.

Craig, then 23 years old, was the model of patience in the 100-meter dash. As the finalists took their marks, one after another kept false-starting. Each time, Craig would burst out of his starting position with them. In fact, one time he raced the length of the track before he was recalled for another start. On the eighth start, the runners ran for good. Tired but undaunted, Craig dashed to the tape in 10.8 seconds, a tenth of a second faster than his two American teammates. Later, in the 200-meter dash, Craig didn't have such a hectic start, but the finish was just as tough as he once again won by a mere tenth of a second.

Craig had reached the end of the line in Olympic track—but he was far from the end of the line in Olympic competition. Thirty-six years from it, to be exact.

As he pursued a profession as an industrial engineer, he dabbled in many sports. Then, at age 59, he was on an Olympic roster again.

In 1948 at London, Craig was a crew member of the U.S. Olympic yacht *Rhythm*, in the dragon class.

Rhythm didn't move as fast as Craig's legs had in 1912, so the yacht and its crew finished only eleventh. But Ralph Craig's "comeback" after 36 years is believed to have set some kind of Olympic record in its own right.

1920–1936 ICE HOCKEY
Canada Ruled the World in Flawless Fashion

Everyone knows that ice hockey is Canada's game. So naturally, the country where the game was given its birth and development should rule the Olympic version of the game, too. However, the best Canadian hockey players turn professional and therefore are ineligible to compete.

But that drawback did not hurt the Canadians when the game was fostered through its early years in the Olympics. For four Olympics and most of another the Canadians did not lose a game. When they finally saw their 20-game unbeaten string (with one tie) come to an end, it was hardly fair to pin them with defeat. The team that beat them was Great Britain, which had a squad that included ten British-born but Canadian-reared and Canadian-trained players.

Canada's first gold medal in ice hockey actually came in the Summer Olympics, not the Winter Games. The sport was put on the agenda of the 1920 Olympics at Antwerp,

Belgium, because there were no Winter Games until 1924. Canada swept the field.

In 1924, the Canadians ran away from their early opponents by astronomical scores; in four games, they scored 104 goals to their opponents' two. Their foe for the finals was a U.S. team that had a 72-0 goals-for-and-against record. The Americans scored against Canada in the first period, but after that the Canadians took control and won, 6-1.

The Canadians were so far superior to the rest of the world, even using just their amateurs, that the team was asked to skip the preliminary round of the 1928 tournament and just play in the final round. This they did, reluctantly, and still lambasted the best of the field by 11-0, 14-0, and 13-0 scores. The team continued to waltz through Olympic competition in 1932. Going into the 1936 finale against the Canadian-laden British team, the high-scoring Canadian nationals rolled up seven victories and tallied 52 goals to their opponents' 5.

But a British-born, Canadian-trained goalie named Jimmy Foster cut their unbeaten streak short. He was even stingier than the Canadian goalie, having allowed just two goals in six games. He gave up only one goal to the Canadians, and his team won, 2-1. After that, Canada won Olympic titles two more times before the Russians moved in on their game in 1956.

THE 14-GAME UNBEATEN STREAK, 1920-1936

1920 Olympics at Antwerp, Belgium
Canada 15, Czechoslovakia 0
Canada 2, United States 0
Canada 12, Sweden 1

1924 Olympics at Chamonix, France
Canada 30, Czechoslovakia 0
Canada 22, Sweden 0
Canada 33, Switzerland 0

Canada 19, England 2
Canada 6, United States 1

1928 Olympics at St. Moritz, Switzerland
Canada 11, Sweden 0
Canada 14, Great Britain 0
Canada 13, Switzerland 0

1932 Olympics at Lake Placid, New York
Canada 2, United States 1 (overtime)
Canada 4, Germany 1
Canada 9, Poland 0
Canada 5, Germany 0
Canada 10, Poland 0
Canada 2, United States 2 (tie)

1936 Olympics at Garmisch, Germany
Canada 8, Poland 1
Canada 11, Latvia 0
Canada 5, Austria 2
Great Britain 2, Canada 1

1920 SHOOTING
Oscar Swahn Won a Medal at Age 73

The Olympics used to include an event called "Running Deer" in the shooting category, and it was this event that produced one of the oldest gold medal winners. He was Oscar Swahn, a Swede, who won the title at London in 1908 when he was 61.

But Swahn's aim remained accurate, much to the running deer's displeasure. In 1920, when he was 73, Swahn picked up a silver medal in the same event at Antwerp. That, according to all available Olympic archives, made Swahn the oldest medal winner ever. No one has surpassed his feat.

Swahn may have been the oldest man to win a medal. But he wasn't the oldest person ever to receive one. That distinction, because of a technicality, belongs to an American named Anders Haugen.

When Haugen was 36 years old and representing the United States in the first Winter Olympics at Chamonix,

France, he left after the Games thinking he was a fourth-place finisher. That wasn't bad considering that no Americans won ski medals in those initial Winter Games. At least Haugen, a pioneer member of the Lake Tahoe, California, Ski Club, had come closer than his teammates.

But Haugen was even closer than he figured.

Fifty years later, while the triumphant Norwegian ski team was celebrating its fiftieth anniversary, one of the stars was combing through the old statistics and came across a discrepancy. It showed that the scores had been added incorrectly and that another jumper had mistakenly been given the bronze medal. The man who found the error, two-time silver medalist Thorlaf Stromstad, reported it in early 1974 as a gesture of goodwill.

Haugen, still alive at 86, was rightly awarded his bronze. In getting it, he retroactively became the first American to earn a skiing medal.

1920 BOXING, 1932 BOBSLED
Eddie Eagan's Second Gold Was Tougher than His First

Nobody denies that boxing is one of man's toughest physical sports, but the 1920 Olympic light-heavyweight champion found out that there are tougher things to do in sports.

Eddie Eagan, an American, showed that he knew the skills of boxing quite well, but he knew nothing about a bobsled when he ventured to Lake Placid, New York, for the 1928 Winter Games. That did not deter Eagan from asking for a spot on the U.S. four-man team, however. He figured that as an ex-fighter he was tough enough and that as a Yale and Oxford man he was smart enough to know what he was doing.

Bobsledding officials figured they would be smart, too, and asked Eagan to sign a letter which would make them not responsible for any mishap he might become involved in. Eagan agreed.

In practice sessions down icy runways with 80-degree

banks, Eagan furthered his education. For once in his life, he was frightened to death. He tore down the track at treacherous speeds and watched what seemed to be continuous walls of white on both sides of him each time he dared sneak a peek. His head snapped back and forth with each darting change of direction, and he became dizzy from the movement. Here was a man who had never feared speed before, but later he had to admit he had never before experienced this kind of speed. For about two minutes, he clutched onto the bobsled straps while his heart pounded away. Scared, but not scared off, he decided to stay on with the bobsledders, and he did indeed earn a berth on the Americans' No. 1 sled.

A few weeks later, he was in that sled roaring down the track for 7 minutes 53.68 seconds in actual Games competition. Bunched in the second position, he did his job—and earned a gold medal. He thus became the only person to win golds at both the Summer and Winter Olympics.

1924 ICE HOCKEY
Harry Watson Went beyond the "Hat Trick"

The "hat trick" is ice hockey's measure of a good game by a scorer—three goals in a game. Harry Watson, a member of the championship Canadian team in the 1924 Olympics, went beyond the hat trick in his team's wild 30–0 victory over Czechoslovakia. Before the game was over, he had a total of 13 goals, a collection a lot of players would like to have for an entire Olympic tournament.

According to Lefty Reid, editor of the Hockey Hall of Fame's annual guide, *Hockey's Heritage*, that's probably the Olympic record. No official records are kept for individuals in the Olympic tournaments.

1924 TRACK AND FIELD
Paavo Nurmi–Willie Ritola Rivalry Helped the Finns

Perhaps no Olympic rivalry was more bitter than the intrasquad disdain that Finnish distance stars Paavo Nurmi and Willie Ritola had for each other in the 1920s. They were the greatest runners of their time, and they completely dominated the longer running events for nearly a decade.

Ritola won five gold medals (three individual, two team) and four silvers. Nurmi was even better, with nine golds (seven of them individual) and three silvers. In fact, Nurmi won more track and field medals than any other man.

But Nurmi and Ritola didn't particularly like to share the glory with each other. Each wanted it for himself. Their rivalry came to a head in 1924.

Nurmi had won the Olympic 10,000-meter run in the 1920 Games, shortly before Ritola emerged as an outstanding international runner. In 1924, an Olympic year, Nurmi held world records at six different distances between 1,500 and 10,000 meters. No one doubted that the "Flying Finn," as he was called, could win just about any distance event he wanted to.

But no matter how great he proved himself, for some strange reason Finnish authorities would not let him enter the 10,000-meter event in the 1924 Games. He would be listed for the 1,500 and 5,000 and team events. The 10,000 would be reserved for Ritola, the up-and-coming star.

On July 6, Ritola did run and win, as expected. Since he broke the world record by 12.2 seconds on a saturated track in Paris, there could be no doubt about his ability. Three days later, he won the 3,000-meter steeplechase, again in world record time as he led a 1-2-3 sweep by the Finns.

Meanwhile, Nurmi was qualifying for his big day—July 10. The organizers of the 1924 Olympics had scheduled the 1,500 and 5,000 runs just 25 minutes apart. That caused a howl from Finnish officials who felt it was an insult to their great runners, particularly Nurmi, who wanted to double up. So the organizers relented slightly, and rescheduled the finals 55 minutes apart, which still wasn't a reasonable time span.

Ritola, eager and as energetic as Nurmi, was also scheduled for the 5,000, which would give him a chance to outdo his rival if he could clinch another gold medal. Nurmi didn't concentrate on the 1,500 much after he learned about his upcoming showdown with Ritola in the 5,000.

On July 10, Nurmi started out his 1,500 with his stopwatch in hand to measure his pace. After 1,000 meters, however, his blistering pace had left the opposition far behind, so he tossed his watch to trackside and coasted home to win easily in 3:53.6, an Olympic record. He could have broken the world record had he tried.

But Nurmi's thoughts were centered on the 5,000. He had less than an hour to prepare.

In the 5,000 race, Ritola and another runner ran way out in front, over 30 meters ahead of Nurmi. The idea, it seemed, was to try to break him since he had just completed the other race. Nurmi, however, stayed close to his prerace plan, studying his stopwatch instead of the opposition.

Not quite halfway through the race, Nurmi worked his way into the lead. Ritola stayed with him, and the two left the other runners strung out far behind. The two went to the stretch run together, and now it was time for Nurmi to forget his watch and race to the tape. He got there first, in 14:31.2, with Ritola just two-tenths of a second behind. The rest of the field trailed by a half minute.

Nurmi had made Olympic history which will probably never be repeated because of modern scheduling: two gold medals in races that began less than an hour apart.

But his battle with Ritola was not over. Each had two golds, and Ritola had a silver besides. In consecutive days, they would run 3,000-meter team race (not a relay) heats, a 10,000-meter cross-country final and the 3,000-meter team final.

Nurmi left Ritola behind in each match, but between them they helped Finland get two more gold medals.

After the Games came to an end, Nurmi set out to break Ritola's world record in the 10,000. He did it on August 31, shattering it by over 17 seconds. But again, it was Finland as a nation that derived the benefits, as well as the individual runner.

1924 TRACK AND FIELD
Bob Le Gendre Was a Jump Ahead of the Olympics

How can one break a world record in the Olympics, and not set an Olympic record? Read on—it actually happened in 1924.

Bob Le Gendre was one of America's better long jumpers in the early 1920s, but his Olympic hopes in 1924 were built around the pentathlon event. The pentathlon, which was discontinued after the 1924 Olympics, was somewhat of a minidecathlon, made up of five events—the 200-meter dash, the 1,500-meter run, the javelin throw, the discus throw, and the long jump. It was the event in which Jim Thorpe had won one of his two gold medals in his famed 1912 Olympic appearance. But the pentathlon was also one of track and field's lesser lights, and that's why it was dropped.

The Olympic crowd at Paris on July 7, 1924, was paying little attention to the pentathlon competition. A world record run in the 400-meter hurdles and the upset of Charlie Paddock in the 100-meter dash caused a commotion that stirred up the fans. Besides, the long-jump portion of the pentathlon was held on the side of the track, far away from the core of the spectators.

The pentathletes themselves began to huddle around the jumping pit, though, after Le Gendre, a former Georgetown University star, leaped 24 feet 10 1/4 inches on his first try (of three attempts). That was only an inch off the Olympic record. It also was a personal best for Le Gendre, who had been the Amateur Athletic Union and National Collegiate Athletic Association champ in 1922. Le Gendre got off another fine jump—24 feet even—on his second try.

Then he leaped into the record books on his last attempt, going 25 feet 5 3/4 inches. That was better than the Olympic record by a good margin and almost 3 inches better than the world mark set by his American teammate, Ned Gourdin, in 1921.

The jump earned Le Gendre the world record because it was set in bona fide track and field competition. That was not denied. But he could not get credit for an Olympic long-jump record because it was not made in the regular long-jump competition.

The next day, the regular long jumpers took the field, and an American, DeHart Hubbard, won the event at 24 feet 5 inches. Gourdin was second. Meanwhile, Le Gendre, who had leaped a foot better than the Olympic champ, could earn no more than a bronze medal for his pentathlon efforts.

Hubbard and Gourdin would have their days, though. In fact, Gourdin's came the very next day, when he jumped 25 feet 8 inches. Unfortunately, it was for the benefit of cameramen, and not in competition, so it didn't count. Hubbard had to wait a year, but he eventually became the world record holder with a mark of 25 feet 10 7/8 inches.

The decathlon competition at Paris that year also produced an oddity. The winner was Harold Osborne, an American from Illinois who also won the high jump at 6 feet 6 inches, an Olympic record. No other man has ever won both the decathlon and another individual event.

1924 SWIMMING AND DIVING
Aileen Riggin Achieved a Unique Aquatic Double

Swimming and diving seem to go together like hand and glove, but not so in Olympic competition. Though they are grouped together like track and field, the two are entirely different sports when it comes to competitive skills.

Yet 17-year-old Aileen Riggin of the U.S. Olympic team managed to win medals in individual events in both swimming and diving in 1924.

As a pint-sized 13-year-old Olympian in 1920, Aileen Riggin had won the first springboard diving (then called "fancy diving") event held for women in the Games. She was the youngest girl to win an Olympic medal up to that time.

Being a pretty good swimmer after she hit the water, she decided to try for a rare double in 1924 at Paris. She made the U.S. team both as a springboard diver and as a backstroker.

She didn't quite defend her diving title, but she did come

in second and collect a silver medal. Then in the first 100-meter women's backstroke held in Olympic competition, she paddled her way to third place for a bronze medal.

Katherine Rawls, one of the great women athletes in American history, might have come even closer to Riggin's goal of gold medals in both swimming and diving if the Olympics in the 1930s had had the same swimming format that they do now.

Miss Rawls was a diver good enough to win silver medals at both Los Angeles in 1932 and Berlin in 1936 for her springboard diving. She was only 14 when she won the first of those medals, and it was only her first international competition.

In 1932, she was already a standout swimmer, having won two national championships. But her best event—the individual medley—wasn't on the Olympic agenda as it is nowadays. Katherine waited until 1936 to try to duplicate Aileen's swimming-diving double. She made the team easily as a diver and also earned a chance to go after a swimming medal when she qualified in the 100-meter freestyle.

At Berlin, however, she finished only seventh among the freestylers. But as a result of being one of the best Americans in that event, she got to swim with the relay team, too. The United States finished third, which enabled her to take home a bronze medal.

She continued to improve as a swimmer to the point where she had won more American championships than any other woman. Unfortunately, World War II wiped out the 1940 Olympics and her chance to match Aileen Riggin's double.

1924–1936 FIGURE SKATING
Sonja Henie Went from Last to First

The last-place finisher in the women's figure skating at the 1924 Olympics received more attention than is generally reserved for an athlete at the bottom end of the scoring tables. But this tail-ender was different.

For one thing, she wasn't a woman; she was an 11-year-old girl. And her routine, even if it didn't score highly with the official scorers, registered with the spectators. Fair-haired, cherubic Sonja Henie's Olympic debut was a success in every category except the scoring. She had begun to change figure skating from the rigid, methodical sport it had been to the free-flowing, artistic success it is today.

The daughter of an Oslo fur dealer, Miss Henie grew up with an appreciation of the arts. But her Scandinavian upbringing also sent her outdoors to appreciate winter sports. As a small child she practiced ballet. Then at age 6, when she was given ice skates as a gift, she combined the two pastimes. By age 10, she was the Norwegian national figure-skating champion.

The scoring system in the 1924 Olympics had a lot to do with her tail-end finish. School figures rather than the free skating that she tried to introduce took precedence. The spectators then, as they do now, enjoyed the free skating more. The judges reexamined their scoring systems after hearing the applause she got.

Four years later, at St. Moritz, Switzerland, she danced her way to the Olympic crown by a sizeable margin.

With higher jumps, longer spins, and daring routines, she won over the crowds at the Olympics and at international championships. She was easily the best as well as the most exciting figure skater to come along.

Sonja Henie repeated her Olympic championship in 1932 at Lake Placid, New York, and in 1936 at Garmisch in the Bavarian Alps. By 1936, she was only 24 years old and could have gone on competing for years. But there was no competition left for her; she had widened the gap by continuing to improve.

No woman had ever won gold medals in three consecutive Olympics before in any sport. And no one has won more than one in figure skating since Miss Henie retired, which she did after 1936. Sonja left competitive skating but she continued to glide gracefully over the rinks for millions of movie and ice revue fans.

1932–1960 FENCING
Aladar Gerevich Was Sharp for Six Olympics

When 22-year-old Aladar Gerevich won a gold medal in the 1932 Games for his role on Hungary's sabre fencing team, he didn't realize what he was starting.

Despite a World War that wiped out two Olympics (the 1940 and 1944 Games), Gerevich continued to compete until he won golds as a member of the sabre squad six consecutive times. No other athlete has won golds in six straight Olympics, or six different Olympics, for that matter. (The only man to come close was Gerevich's teammate Paul Kovacs, who was a member of the team from 1936 through 1960, thus giving Kovacs five straight.)

In addition to his team titles, Gerevich won the individual sabre event in 1948. He was a bronze winner in 1936 and a silver medalist in 1952, when he lost to Kovacs. He won ten Olympic medals in all, and Kovacs won nine.

1936 TRACK AND FIELD
Jesse Owens's Records Were Made to Last

The true test of a record in track and field is not its time or distance or height, but rather its durability. Man has gotten stronger and faster as the years go by due to improved nutrition, better equipment, and numerous other factors too obvious to itemize here. Thus it should not be surprising that a quick check of the Olympic archives shows that few records last for more than a four-year period or two Olympiads at best. Going into the 1976 Games at Montreal, no men's record was older than some of those set in 1968.

Therefore, the achievements of Jesse Owens, so well documented in sports history, can be scrutinized in even one more way: When Jesse left his mark on the record book, he left it there for some time.

Owens's feat of winning four gold medals at the 1936 Olympics at Berlin was one of the greatest showings in the modern Games. He won the 100 meters in record-tying time, smashed the 200-meter record, and got the U.S. 400-meter relay team off to such a fine start that it too gave

Jesse a share of another Olympic (and world) best. But it was Jesse's accomplishment in the long jump that stood the test of time.

Owens preferred running to jumping. Even so, his springy legs that were catapulted by his blazing speed down the runways made him invincible. As a high school boy in Cleveland, Ohio, in 1933, he once jumped 24 feet 11¼ inches. That was only 5 inches shy of the Olympic record of the time. That same year he became the Amateur Athletic Union's national men's champion in the event. The following season, as a freshman at Ohio State University, he came under the careful guidance of Coach Larry Snyder. The coach spotted all sorts of flaws in Jesse's jumping technique—he didn't run far enough, he had a hitch as he glided through the air, etc. Snyder got Jesse to lengthen his approach to the jumping board and to refine his flight by practicing his leap over a hurdle. Before the winter season was over, Owens owned the world indoor record on the basis of a 25-foot 3¼-inch jump in New York City.

Owens continued to jump brilliantly even though his talents were also spread over the sprints, the low hurdles, and the relays. Despite his lack of exceptional size, the 160-pound Owens had inner strength that enabled him to compete in several events in the same meet. His versatility was displayed in Ann Arbor, Michigan, in May 1935, when he set three world records and tied another on the same day—within a 45-minute period! One of those records was in the long jump, where he leaped 26 feet 8¼ inches in his only attempt of the day.

Jesse's goal was to make the U.S. Olympic team in 1936. With his talent, that was no problem. He made the team for four different events, including the relay.

His performances at Berlin are noted on the accompanying chart. He sprinted greater than any man ever had, but still it was in his least-liked event—the long jump—where he performed best.

The man who was to give Jesse his stiffest opposition was a handsome blond German named Luz Long, who perfectly fit Adolf Hitler's physical description of "Aryan superiority." But Long did not share Hitler's disdain for the black Americans on the U.S. team.

In fact, it was Long who came to Jesse's aid at a time when he needed it most. Owens had to clear only 23 feet 5½ inches to qualify for the finals. For him, that was a jump he had made early in his high school career. Now he was a 26-footer. But Owens was cited for a foul on the first of his three attempts when he dashed up the runway in his sweatsuit to recheck his steps. The judge counted it as an attempt. His steps still not right, he was 2 inches over the board on his next attempt and again had a foul. Another foul and he would be out.

It was then that Long came forth and offered a suggestion. "You should be able to qualify with your eyes closed," said the German, who had made the distance easily. He then said that Jesse ought to pick a spot to jump from a few inches in front of the board and thus avoid a foul. Owens did, and drew a spot about a foot in front of the board. On his final try he qualified by the barest of margins.

As fate would have it, Owens and his new friend dueled to the end in the finals. Owens regained his timing and jumped over 25 feet on each of his first three tries. In a "believe it or not" double comeback, Long tied Jesse twice—first at 25 feet 4¾ inches, then at 25 feet 9¾ inches on his fifth and next-to-last attempt. One such tie is rare enough; two defies all odds. But Jesse kept coming back strong himself and jumped 26 feet ½ inch to take the lead on his next-to-last jump. Then he clinched the victory with an Olympic record 26-feet 5¼-inch burst.

It has been said that Jesse may have had a better jump that day after the competition ended when he returned to the runway at the request of photographers and went through the motions for them. Experts swear the now loose and lithe Owens made a leap that had to be about 27 feet, but it was unofficial and went unmeasured.

Owens's official jump of 26 feet 5¼ inches was good enough, though. That record was not broken until 1960, when another American, Ralph Boston, jumped 26 feet 7¾ inches. (Ironically, Boston earlier that year wiped out Jesse's world record, too. And more ironically, Boston's Olympic coach was Larry Snyder.)

Owens's Olympic mark had lasted for 24 years. True, there were no Games in the war years of 1940 and 1944. But it withstood the onslaught of the great athletes of the late 1940s and the 1950s. Next to Jesse's 24-year-old record, the longest-standing Olympic men's track record was 16 years—the 5,000-meter run record by Russia's Vladimar Kuts, which was set in 1956 and broken in 1972.

As for Jesse's other Olympic records at Berlin, the 10.3-second 100-meter dash was tied often, but not broken until 1960. His 20.7 time in the 200 was tied in 1952 but not broken until 1956. And the relay record that he shared with his American teammates held until 1956. No wonder this wonder has often been called the greatest Olympian of modern times.

JESSE OWENS'S OLYMPIC "LOG"

Event	Result	Comment
August 2		
100 heat	1st, 10.3 sec.	Wind-aided; otherwise tied Olympic record
100 quarterfinal	1st, 10.2 sec.	Again wind-aided; otherwise world record
August 3		
100 semifinal	1st, 10.4 sec.	
100 final	1st, 10.3 sec.	Equaled Olympic record

44 / Incredible Olympic Feats

Event	Result	Comment
August 4		
200 heat	1st, 21.1 sec.	Broke Olympic record
Long jump (qual.)	Foul, foul, 23' 5$^9/_{16}$"	
200 quarterfinal	1st, 21.1 sec.	Wind-aided
Long-jump final	25' 4$^3/_4$", 25' 9$^3/_4$", 25' 5$^1/_4$", foul, 26' $^1/_2$", 26' 5$^1/_4$"	Bettered Olympic record on all five legal jumps
August 5		
200 semifinal	1st, 21.3 sec.	Eased up in race
200 final	1st, 20.7 sec.	Olympic record
August 8		
400 relay heat	1st, 40.0 sec.	U.S. team tied world record, broke Olympic record
400 relay final	1st, 39.8	U.S. broke world, Olympic records

1936 TRACK
The "Black Auxiliaries" Chased Hitler out of His Stadium

Jesse Owens's superiority in a track uniform was a sight unto itself. But the biggest story to come out of the Berlin Olympics other than Owens's results involved Jesse and his race—that is, his color, not his speed.

The Nazi propaganda machine that was revved to a peak in the 1930s had made a major point of "Aryan superiority." To Adolf Hitler that meant "white power." Blacks had done well for American and Canadian teams for years of Olympic competition, and on the 1936 U.S. men's track and field team they were well represented. About one-seventh of all the U.S. trackmen were blacks. The Nazi propaganda machine had been prepared well in advance to try to stem this black tide at the Nazi's showcase Olympics.

A Nazi-supported newspaper kept referring to these athletes as "America's Black Auxiliaries" and some so-called experts predicted that the Games would put the blacks in their place—and not first place, either.

Owens's talents were internationally known. And he did

46 / Incredible Olympic Feats

not let anybody down with his record-breaking sweep of the 100 meters, 200 meters, long jump, and leadoff leg of the 400-meter relay. But a real second story emerged with the ultrasuccess of Jesse's black teammates.

As Hitler, Goering, Goebbels, Himmler, and many other top Nazis sat in embarrassed awe day after day at the 120,000-seat Berlin Olympic Stadium, the black Americans put on a smashing performance.

Ralph Metcalfe, who nearly won the 100-meter run at Los Angeles in 1932, followed Owens across the finish line of the 100 for another silver medal. Then he collected a gold medal in the 400-meter relay when he teamed with Owens.

Mack Robinson, whose brother Jackie made sports history in his own right years later, finished second to Owens in the 200.

Archie Williams, a Californian, sped to first in the 400-meter dash, with another black teammate, Jim LuValle, a close third for the bronze medal.

A University of Pittsburgh freshman and the youngest of the U.S. black contingent, John Woodruff, trailed for most of the 800-meter race, but roared out of last place near the finish for another impressive gold.

The blacks had now won all the running events from 100 through 800 meters, and shared half of the relay victory. They almost had a victory in the 110-meter high hurdles, too, but Fred Pollard, Jr., geared down after a fast start and finished third, with the same time as the second-place runner.

In the high-jump pit, the American hopefuls were Corny Johnson and Dave Albritton, the latter a teammate of Jesse's from Ohio State. Both were black. Johnson almost missed the finals after getting tied up in Berlin traffic. An American official held up the event as long as he could, but was forced to begin without Johnson.

When Corny got there, the bar was already at 6 feet 6 inches, higher than the Olympic record. But the lithe

Olympic veteran, who had made the team in 1932 as a 17-year-old, calmly cleared the height without the benefit of a warm-up. He continued to jump without a miss until the bar reached 6 feet 7⅞ inches. He made that height, too, on his first attempt and earned himself a gold medal. Teammate Albritton was out at 6 feet 6¾, but that was good enough for a silver. Hitler couldn't stand the sight of Johnson on the winning stand, accepting his gold medal, and stormed out of the stadium without as much as a little applause for the "Black Auxiliaries" who had upset his grandiose plans.

The nine black Americans, who came from all parts of the country—the East, the Midwest, the West—had claimed eight gold medals, three silver, and two bronze for their combined efforts. That was better than the combined results of the rest of their 55 male American teammates. But it also was better than the entire German team, or any other national team. Hitler had suffered his first defeat—to an "enemy" he wanted badly to defeat.

1936 TRACK AND FIELD
Hermann Ratjin Almost Pulled an Upset for *Der Fuehrer*

The legend of the ancient Olympic Games includes a story about how a mother dressed up like a man so she could watch her son compete in the males-only Olympics of the time. Females weren't even allowed in the stadiums as spectators.

Hermann Ratjin wasn't exactly a men's libber when he competed in the 1936 Olympics—the contests Hitler wanted to use so badly to prove his Nordic superiority theories. Since Hermann could jump only a few inches over 5 feet, he obviously didn't belong in the men's high jump, where 6 feet 6 inches or so would be needed to win. So the Nazis put him in the competition where he could do best—the women's high jump.

Hermann, a former waiter who had been competing in women's high jumps for some time under the name Dora Ratjin, was the favorite to take the gold medal at Berlin. But Ibolya, Dorothy, and Elfriede beat him out.

Hermann/Dora came close, though. First, second, and third places went to Ibolya Csak of Hungary, Dorothy Odam of Great Britain, and Elfriede Kaun of Germany. All jumped 5 feet 3 inches—and Csak won the jumpoff. Just a shade behind the medal winners was Herman/Dora, in fourth place.

The hoax was kept a secret from the world for almost three decades.

1936 DIVING
Marjorie Gestring Took Her Doll to the Games and Took a Medal Home

She was called "a minnow" by the sportswriters and the fans for the way her little body cut into the water with hardly a splash after making a dive. She giggled like the schoolgirl she was, carried a doll around with her, and wore a black tank suit which made her appear to be one of the swimmers rather than a diver.

But the tanned, blond Californian made a big hit at Berlin for more than just her appearance at the 1936 Games. Marjorie Gestring, age 13 years and 9 months, went into the competition in full force.

The American men divers had gone 1-2-3 the day before, and Miss Gestring, along with Katherine Rawls and Dorothy Hill wanted to match their sweep in the women's springboard diving on August 12. Miss Rawls, age 19, had won a silver medal four years before when she was only 15. She was considered the favorite for the event. Mrs. Hill, age 22, was considered a better diver than her fellow Los

Angeles teammate, Marjorie, if for no other reason than experience.

Miss Rawls held a narrow 0.4-point lead after the compulsory dives. And she maintained exactly that margin after two of the three voluntary dives. But Marjorie was coming on strong.

Marjorie's first voluntary dive earned her a score of 16.40 that put her temporarily ahead of Rawls. It had been a well-executed half gainer. But the second dive—a 1½ somersault—gave her only 14.40 points and cost her the lead.

Marjorie chose a difficult 1½ backward somersault for her final attempt. Though it was a tough routine to perform, a successful dive would give her more points under the system used in diving. Marjorie slid beautifully into the water, like a minnow, and understood right away that she had executed the dive with great skill. She was laughing when she bobbed out of the water. The judges gave her a 16.00 score. Meanwhile, Rawls scored only 14.94 on her last attempt. Marjorie was the winner by less than 1 point and led an American 1-2-3 sweep in the springboard diving for the fifth straight Olympics.

But more important, she became the youngest winner ever in an individual Olympic event. Nobody has undercut her since.

Divers come in all ages. Hjalmar Johansson of Sweden had to wait until he was 35 to get his first opportunity for a gold medal because there was no platform event until 1908. Johansson won a special 5-meter dive (since discontinued) in 1912. His wife Greta won the first gold medal for women's diving in those 1912 Games in their native Sweden.

1936 SHOOTING
Willy Rogeberg Was a Shooting Star

Taking dead aim at an Olympic gold medal, Willy Rogeberg left no room for error with his small-bore rifle at the 1936 Olympics.

The Norwegian marksman had 30 shots at a 50-meter target with his .22 caliber rifle. He made the best of them, hitting the bullseye each time. His perfect score of 300 was the first ever witnessed in any kind of competition.

The performance not only earned him a gold medal, but set a world's record for the small-bore event.

1936–1972 BASKETBALL
The Americans Were Good at Their Own Game

When the American basketball team won a forfeit from civil war-plagued Spain in the 1936 Olympic basketball opener, no one really paid much attention. But the 2–0 victory (that's the score posted in a basketball forfeit) turned out to be very significant, if not outright ironic. That was the first year the American-invented game was played in the Olympics, and it wouldn't be until 1972's finale that any team would get closer to the Americans in their final scores.

With the forfeit victory, the American teams over the years rang up 63 straight victories for one of the greatest feats in the history of the Games. Certainly no country in any other team sport won more consistently.

In 1948, the Argentines came within 2 points of the U.S. cagers, before losing 59–57. Brazil held the margin of defeat to 4 points in 1952. But of America's 63 straight triumphs, only seven times did opponents get within 10 points. The

U.S. players were so overpowering that they topped 100 points 12 times during the streak and more than doubled the score on their hapless foes on 20 occasions.

The first Olympic basketball tournament in 1936 was pretty much a walkaway for the American team. The Canadians tried holding the ball in the final game—played outdoors on a wet, muddy court—but all that did was result in Canada scoring only 8 points itself. The Americans won, 19–8.

The U.S. players were so talented in that first tourney that the Japanese proposed, and almost got through, a rule at the international basketball federation's meeting that would have limited the height of players to 1.90 meters (6 feet 2¾ inches).

The next time the Olympics were played, in 1948 after World War II, the Americans showed up in London with a 6-foot 11-inch center named Bob Kurland, who dominated the tournament. The rugged graduate of Oklahoma A&M had a lot of support from the players from the outstanding University of Kentucky team—Alex Groza, Ralph Beard, "Wah Wah" Jones, and others. Except for their 2-point victory over Argentina, every game was a runaway.

When 7-foot University of Kansas star Clyde Lovelette joined Kurland for the 1952 Games, another howl of protest could be heard about heights of players. This time, a 6-foot 4¾-inch limit was requested but refused. The protesters probably wanted the restrictions even more after watching Kurland and Lovelette play. They were the high scorers in all but one of their eight games.

The 1956 team featured Bill Russell, who was used to taking part in winning streaks. His University of San Francisco quintet had won 59 games in a row while he was there, and he was about to join the professional Boston Celtics and become the pivotal figure in their dynasty that lasted for over a decade.

Russell's forte was defense, even though he was a shorter

center at about 6 feet 9 inches. But he still topped the U.S. squad in scoring at Melbourne with a 14.1 average. The Americans dominated the playoffs to the extent that no one came within 30 points of beating them. They knocked off one opponent by 72 points and four others by 58 or more.

Perhaps no team in basketball—amateur, Olympic, or professional—ever had as much raw talent as the 1960 U.S. squad. Made up mostly from a bumper crop of great collegians, the team included Oscar Robertson, Jerry West, Jerry Lucas, Walt Bellamy, Terry Dischinger, Adrian Smith, Darrall Imhoff, and Bob Boozer, all of whom would star in the professional ranks for a decade or more. The team averaged over 100 points. When Coach Pete Newell pulled his top stars such as Lucas, Robertson, and West out of games as an act of mercy to opponents, the players on the bench would come in fresh and make life even more miserable. Though basketball in the world was improving at a fast rate, the Americans polished off their opponents by margins ranging from 24 to 59 points.

"This was the greatest team I have ever seen," said Brazil's star Walmir Marques, who had played in the 1956 Olympics too.

The 1964 American squad may not have matched its 1960 counterparts in overall talent, but it was made up of the right blend of physical and polished players. The most polished was Princeton University's All-American Bill Bradley, who pulled the team together. He and Walt Hazzard were the ball-handling wizards, while Jim Barnes, Mel Counts, Lucius Jackson, and Joe Caldwell gave the team rebounding superiority.

In 1968, the Americans were finally predicted to go under for the first time. It wasn't that the fountain of talent had run out in the United States. It's just that the best players didn't make themselves available. Elvin Hayes, Wes Unseld, and Lew Alcindor would have dominated any Olympic field, but for various reasons they refused to go to

Mexico City with the U.S. squad. The Americans wound up with a makeshift team that included one player who was the third best man on his college team, and another who was only the fifth best. For the first time, the Americans went to the Games without an established superstar.

For a center, a 19-year-old junior college player, Spencer Haywood, was selected. He was the first "juco" to be picked for an American team, which showed how far down the ranks the United States was reaching. And he was only 6 feet 9 inches, which didn't seem much of a threat to opposing teams, who no longer were bemoaning the height of Americans because they had tall players of their own.

The reaction to Haywood's selection was lack of interest at best. Any American fan knew that Alcindor, Hayes, or Unseld would almost guarantee a gold medal. But not "Spencer Who," as the sportswriters called him.

By the time the 1968 Games were over, Spencer Haywood was just as much a household name in the United States as the three absentees. He led the team in scoring in six of nine games and swept the backboards clean of rebounds night after night. His defense was tenacious. He symbolized the team's spirit with his V-for-victory signs after each big play. It was Haywood's 21 big points and all-around heroics that enabled the United States to defeat Yugoslavia, 65–50, in the final game and keep the winning streak intact.

Haywood's 147 points was a record for individual scoring by a U.S. player in the Olympics even though he was the youngest player the Americans had ever chosen to represent them.

The U.S. victory streak now stood at 55. The days of the American runaways in the basketball world were over, but the United States was still the dominant country playing the game. Even though many of the best U.S. prospects were dropping out of college to play for the professional teams by 1972, there was plenty of talent available for an Olympic squad. Ed Ratleff and Tom Henderson gave the United States two talented, capable guards. Doug Collins, like Ratleff, was a 6-foot 6-inch player who could play guard; he was a 30-point scorer in college. Jim Brewer, Dwight Jones, Mike Bantom, and Tommy Burleson gave the team height and strength up front. Burleson's 7-foot 4-inch height was intimidating by itself. Tom McMillen and Bobby Jones were additional polished forwards.

The team was built around defense, and for each of its nine games did a fine job.

But it was a young team (with 8 of 12 players 20 years old or younger) and prone to making mistakes. Only four of the squadmen had any international experience. Opposing players had taken part in as many as 300 games under the international rules, which differ from the U.S. rules for basketball.

Still the Americans held their own. They played a somewhat sloppy game against Cuba, but won out on superior talent in the stretch. They fended off a good Brazil team, and they rolled over some other opponents. When they defeated a good Italian team by 30 points in the semifinal game, they seemed ready to take on the Russians for the gold medal.

The finale was scheduled for 11:30 P.M., Munich time, in order to accommodate television. The Russians accommodated television, too, by taking the lead and holding it for 35 minutes of the 40-minute game. This would be one year when the United States would not waltz through the final game.

Then began the most bizarre finish of any game in basketball history. The Americans, who had been playing poorly, caught up to the Russians and went ahead, 50–49, on Doug Collins' free throws. There were 3 seconds left on the clock.

The Russians did not score, and the Americans joyously celebrated their "victory." Then, they were called back to the court to have the 3 seconds replayed. The "logic" behind the decision went like this: during Collins's free-throw attempts, the Russian coach called for an illegal time-out, which was given to him. So the international official who ran the Games decided that the Russians should get the 3 seconds over! The Russians put the ball in play again at the American end of the court, trying for a desperation basket. They failed, but so did the timing devices. The clock was reset once more—and this time the Russians scored a miraculous basket, which was aided by the Russian player knocking to the floor the two Americans guarding him.

Russia had won, 51–50, and after a 14-hour protest meeting, the Soviets had officially ended the U.S. streak at 63. The American team refused to accept the silver medal.

THE 63-GAME WINNING STREAK
(F indicates final game)

Score	Margin	Leading U.S. Scorer/Points
1936 at Berlin		
U.S. 2, Spain 0 (forfeit)	—	None
U.S. 52, Estonia 28	24	Frank Lubin 13
U.S. 56, Philippines 23	33	Joe Fortenberry 21
U.S. 25, Mexico 10	15	Samuel Balter 10
U.S. 19, Canada 8 (F)	11	Fortenberry 8
1948 at London		
U.S. 86, Switzerland 21	65	Alex Groza 19
U.S. 53, Czechoslovakia 28	25	Vince Boryla 9
U.S. 59, Argentina 57	2	Gordon Carpenter, Don Barksdale 12
U.S. 66, Egypt 28	38	Barksdale 17
U.S. 61, Peru 33	28	W. "Wah Wah" Jones 12
U.S. 63, Uruguay 28	35	Bob Kurland 19
U.S. 71, Mexico 40	31	Groza 19
U.S. 65, France 21 (F)	44	Groza 11
1952 at Helsinki		
U.S. 66, Hungary 48	18	Dan Pippen 15

Score	Margin	Leading U.S. Scorer/Points
U.S. 72, Czechoslovakia 47	25	Bob Kurland 12
U.S. 57, Uruguay 44	13	Kurland 21
U.S. 86, U.S.S.R. 58	28	Kurland 15
U.S. 103, Chile 55	48	Clyde Lovelette 25
U.S. 57, Brazil 53	4	Lovelette 11
U.S. 85, Argentina 76	9	Lovelette 25
U.S. 36, U.S.S.R. 25 (F)	11	Lovelette 9

1956 at Melbourne

Score	Margin	Leading U.S. Scorer/Points
U.S. 98, Japan 40	58	Bill Russell 20
U.S. 101, Thailand 29	72	Ronald Tomsic 15
U.S. 121, Philippines 53	68	Bob Jeangerard 21
U.S. 85, Bulgaria 44	41	Jeangerard 19
U.S. 113, Brazil 51	62	Russell 17
U.S. 85, U.S.S.R. 55	30	Russell 20
U.S. 101, Uruguay 38	63	Tomsic 18
U.S. 89, U.S.S.R. 55 (F)	34	Jeangerard 16

1960 at Rome

Score	Margin	Leading U.S. Scorer/Points
U.S. 88, Italy 54	34	Adrian Smith 17
U.S. 125, Japan 66	59	Jerry Lucas 28
U.S. 107, Hungary 63	44	Oscar Robertson 22
U.S. 104, Yugoslavia	42	Robertson, Terry Dischinger 16
U.S. 108, Uruguay 50	58	Smith 15
U.S. 81, U.S.S.R. 57	24	Jerry West 19
U.S. 112, Italy 81	31	Lucas 26
U.S. 90, Brazil 63 (F)	27	Lucas 23

1964 at Tokyo

Score	Margin	Leading U.S. Scorer/Points
U.S. 78, Australia 45	33	Jerry Shipp 16
U.S. 77, Finland 51	26	Shipp 18
U.S. 60, Peru 45	15	Shipp 18
U.S. 83, Uruguay 28	55	Joe Caldwel 16
U.S. 69, Yugoslavia 61	8	Shipp 22
U.S. 86, Brazil 53	33	Lucius Jackson 17
U.S. 116, Korea 50	66	Jim Barnes 26
U.S. 62, Puerto Rico 42	20	Bill Bradley, Shipp 16
U.S. 73, U.S.S.R. 59 (F)	14	Jackson 17

1968 at Mexico City

Score	Margin	Leading U.S. Scorer/Points
U.S. 81, Spain 46	35	Spencer Haywood 12
U.S. 93, Senegal 36	57	Haywood 16
U.S. 96, Philippines 75	21	Bill Hosket 16
U.S. 95, Panama 60	25	Haywood 27
U.S. 100, Italy 61	39	Haywood 26
U.S. 73, Yugoslavia 58	25	Jo Jo White 24
U.S. 61, Puerto Rico 56	5	Haywood 21
U.S. 75, Brazil 63	12	White 14
U.S. 65, Yugoslavia 50 (F)	15	Haywood 21

Score	Margin	Leading U.S. Scorer/Points
1972 at Munich		
U.S. 66, Czechoslovakia 35	31	Tom Henderson 16
U.S. 81, Australia 55	26	Ed Ratleff 16
U.S. 67, Cuba 48	19	Dwight Jones 18
U.S. 61, Brazil 54	7	Henderson 12
U.S. 96, Egypt 31	65	Mike Bantom 17
U.S. 72, Spain 56	16	Bantom 11
U.S. 99, Japan 33	66	Bantom 18
U.S. 68, Italy 38	30	Jim Forbes 14
U.S.S.R. 51, U.S. 50 (F)	−1	Henderson, Jim Brewer 9

1948 TRACK AND FIELD
Bob Mathias Was the "Boy Wonder" of All Time

At the official opening ceremonies of the Olympics, a bell is rung and the international president of the games announces to an overflow crowd of participants and fans, "I summon the youth of the world." It's one of the more dramatic moments in an athlete's life, but in truth a lot of them don't exactly fit the "youth" mold. Many Olympic champions are well up in their twenties or thirties. It takes a lot of training to qualify to reach the starting line.

The 1948 Olympics had many old-timers, sports veterans who had to wait for a war to finish before they could start their quests for gold medals. But when the 1948 Games came to a conclusion, the "man" who stood out most was 17-year-old Bob Mathias of little Tulare, California.

It was Mathias's first Olympics, naturally. But he handled his task like a veteran.

In June of 1948, the rugged football-basketball-track star took part in a meet in Pasadena in which he ran 100 meters in 11.3 seconds, the 400 in 52.1, the hurdles in 15.7, and the 1,500 meters in 4:59.2. He long-jumped 21 feet 4½ inches, high-jumped 5 feet 10 inches, and pole-vaulted 11 feet 9 inches. He threw the shot 43 feet 1 inch, the discus 140 feet ⅛ inch, and the javelin 175 feet 4⅝ inches.

None of those marks could begin to earn him a place in an individual event at the Olympics tryouts. In fact, it was only his fourth week with a pole vault or a javelin, and several of his marks were personal bests.

But his overall performance won Mathias a surprising first place against some of the better U.S. decathlon men in the Southern Pacific Amateur Athletic Union championships. The rival decathletes were stunned to find out it was Mathias's debut in the grueling event.

Two weeks later, Mathias was in Bloomfield, New Jersey, trying out for the U.S. Olympic team.

On the first of the two-day decathlon trial, Mathias improved in four of his five events. He began the second day with an impressive 15.1-second run through the hurdles. The older competitors were in awe of the 6-foot, 185-pound Mathias's talents. He completed the day with 7,224 decathlon points (under the scoring system at that time). Those points not only got him a victory but represented the highest score since before the war.

He had begun the decathlon training merely two months before, with the complaint that "the more I hear about it, the less I like it." But this high school coach was hoping that the experience in 1948 would help prepare him for the decathlon at the 1952 Olympics. It was never too early to start, reasoned coach Virgil Jackson.

The fast starter was so good, he made the U.S. Olympic team. The Americans, for all their Olympic achievements, had never had a younger member on their men's track squad.

If age seemed against him at Wembly Stadium in London, it did not show. Mathias refused to panic before or after he got there.

On the first day of competition, there was reason for more mature men to fold. But when Bob long-jumped over 23 feet, his best personal record by far, then fell backward to lose the valuable points, he didn't do much more than blink. He later jumped 21 feet 8¼ inches, which gave him far fewer points on the graded scoring table. In his next event, the shot put, he got off a fine 45-foot throw, but fouled. Again he coolly held his head. As the 35 entrants moved over to the high-jump bar, he wasn't in very good standing.

When he twice missed at 5 feet 9 inches, his place in Olympic trivia seemed destined to revolve around the mere fact that he was the youngest U.S. competitor—period. But he cleared 5 feet 9 inches, and later shot up past 6 feet 1¼ inches and was back in the running.

"If I had panicked," he said later, "I would have thrown away what chance I had left on the second day."

As it was, Bob ran the 100 in 11.2 and the 400 in 51.7 and stayed within 49 points of the leader. He was in third place going into the second and final day.

He kept a grip on himself despite more troubles. His hurdle time was 15.7, which was very bad for him. And officials lost his marker after one of his best throws in the discus, so he had to settle for 144 feet 4 inches. The comeback throw pushed him into first place.

In the wet and mud, Mathias had to participate in his worst event—the pole vault. He was hungry and the field was poorly lit for such a technical event. But Mathias vaulted 11 feet 5¾ inches, almost his best height ever. He tried 11 feet 9 inches but didn't take his final attempt for fear of wasting energy needlessly or getting hurt. He would save all his strength for the javelin and the 1,500.

In pouring rain, with just a flashlight to light the foul line, Mathias's first throw was ruled no good. He gave it his best on the second, despite a sore elbow, and threw 165 feet 1 inch. That put him in position to win if he could run a good race in the 1,500.

The 1,500 is a tough event because it comes last on the decathlon agenda, after athletes have spent their bodies in the first nine events. Decathletes aren't usually good distance men, either, so on a graded scale there are few points to be made. But Mathias plowed around the track in a time of 5:11 to gain 354 valuable points. It was enough to also make him the Olympic champion at age 17.

Seventeen years, eight months, and three weeks to be exact.

He vowed that if he lived to be a hundred, he wouldn't try another one. He was too tired, too hungry, too beaten—even though he was a winner.

In little Tulare, the lights burned all night to keep up with his progress. When he finally won, he became their ultimate hero. He was a hero throughout the United States and the world too, and when he found out just how much adulation there was for him, he decided to continue in decathlon competition. Mathias was better than ever at the 1952 Olympics. He improved on each one of his ten London marks and won his gold medal by the largest margin in decathlon history.

Event	Mathias at London	Mathias at Helsinki
100 meters	11.2 sec.*	10.9 sec.
Long jump	21' 8¼"†	22' 10¾"
Shot put	42' 9¼"	50' 2⅜"†
High jump	6' 1¼"*	6' 2⅘"*
400 meters	51.7 sec.	50.2 sec.*
110-meter hurdles	15.7 sec.	14.7 sec.
Discus	144' 4"†	153' 10"
Pole vault	11' 5¾"	13' 1½"†
Javelin	165' 1"	194' 3⅛"
1,500 meters	5:11.0	4:50.8*

*Personal best performance in the event.
†Personal best during decathlon competition.

1948 TRACK AND FIELD
Harrison Dillard Overcame a Hurdle

Harrison Dillard set out in 1948 to prove he was the greatest hurdler of all time. He was well on his way to doing just that when he began vying for a place on the U.S. Olympic team.

Although he was small for a hurdler at 5 feet 10 inches, he made up for it with an adjusted style of clearing the obstacles, and he was acknowledged as the fastest starter the experts had ever seen in the event. No one, just no one, beat Harrison to the first hurdle. And rarely did anyone beat him to the last. In 1946 and 1947, he was ranked the No. 1 hurdler on earth. In 1948, he showed no sign of a letup, winning all 14 of his indoor races and setting a world record outdoors at the Kansas Relays in April. He won that Kansas race by an astounding 10 yards over Clyde Scott, a man who would be good enough to win the silver medal at London a few months later.

By the time Harrison reached Milwaukee, Wisconsin, for the National Amateur Athletic Union meet, he had pushed his winning streak to 82, mostly in the hurdles, though he ran some dashes, too. He had been timed as fast as 13.6 seconds in the 110-meter hurdles, which was way under the existing Olympic record of 14.2.

His confidence bolstered by his string of successes, Dillard decided to try to make the Olympic team in two events—the high hurdles and the 100-meter sprint. It would be a tough assignment, but if he finished in the top four in the 100-meter trials, chances are he would become a member of the American 400-meter relay team, which was a sure bet to win a gold medal.

The AAU meet in Milwaukee was the first step toward the U.S. Olympic trials. If Dillard did well there, he would advance the following week to the final trials in nearby Evanston, Illinois. But the scheduling at the AAU meet would make his goal difficult. He would be forced to run a heat and a final in both the 100-meter dash and the 110-meter hurdles within 67 minutes. He made it through the heats without too much difficulty, then in his third race of the day lost the 100 to Barney Ewell. The hurdle final was his last event of the day, and tired from all the running and redhot competition, Dillard saw his victory string come to an end when he lost to Bill Porter, who had a 14.1 clocking.

Still, the second-place finishes advanced Dillard to the final U.S. Olympic trials.

At Evanston, college and military stars joined the AAU tryout survivors, and the competition was even stiffer. Dillard seemed to be getting a break, though, when he learned that the 100-meter dash and the hurdle trials would be held on separate days.

In the 100, Dillard got through two heats without much problem, then lost out to Ewell and Mel Patton in the final. However, the third place finish guaranteed him a trip to London and a chance to be on the U.S. sprint relay team.

The next day, he would need only another third place to

ensure him a chance to meet the world's best hurdlers later in the Olympics. He could relax, if he wanted.

But Harrison tore out of the starting blocks with his usual blazing speed. He made it to the first hurdle ahead of the field, as usual, but then he hit the hurdle. It knocked him off stride. As he tried to recover between hurdles, he began losing the smoothness and fluidity that made him great. He hit another hurdle, and another. He fell hopelessly behind and finally just came to a stop at the seventh hurdle. His race for even a third place was lost, and he graciously conceded that fact by marching up the track to congratulate Porter, the winner.

He would have to be content with battling the sprinters instead of fending off the hurdlers, where he would have been the clear favorite in London.

In a year when the competition at the Olympics figured to be very good in the short sprint, Dillard's talents were not all that bad. His idol when he was growing up had been another pretty good runner from his Cleveland, Ohio, hometown named Jesse Owens, who had given him his first pair of track spikes. In 1947, Dillard had run the 100 meters in 10.3 seconds, which was just a shade above the world record at the time. And he was ranked ninth in the world that year. But in 1948 he had been mostly a hurdler in his quest for the Olympic title. Sprinting, as usual, had been a sideline.

The field for the 100 at London's Wembley Stadium was a formidable one. It included the 31-year-old Ewell, an amazingly tough competitor despite his age. Then there was Patton, the other American, who was young and a world record setter in 1948 in the 100-yard dash. Patton had broken Jesse Owens's mark when he became the first man to do 9.3 seconds. Also a man to watch was Lloyd LaBeach of Panama, who had shared the 100-yard record with Owens before Patton smashed it.

Despite these men and others, Dillard survived all the

heats and the semifinals and became one of the elite six who would run the July 31 final. Patton, Ewell, LaBeach, and two English runners also advanced.

Dillard drew the outside lane for the race. That wasn't good; it's hard to follow the other sprinters from that vantage point.

Way to the other side of the track in lanes 1, 2, and 3 were the top contenders—Patton, Ewell, and LaBeach. Some 83,000 screaming fans rose to their feet with the pop of the starting gun.

Not surprisingly, Dillard shot out of the blocks faster than anyone. But he did get a break when Patton, a nervous sort despite his enormous talent, got off slowly. Patton picked up speed and LaBeach threatened too, but neither could keep up with Dillard. Ewell, the wise old runner, gained rapidly on him though and lunged through the finish line—his arms up high and jumping for joy.

Ewell had been concentrating his attentions on the two rivals who flanked him, and hardly noticed Dillard way over on the other side of the track.

As Ewell danced around the finish line waiting for congratulations from his foes, Dillard quietly listened for the judges' decision. "Let's wait and see," he calmly told Ewell.

The official announcement was made in short time: "First, Dillard, United States; Time of 10.3, equaling the Olympic record." It was a record shared by his old friend Jesse Owens just to make the day complete.

Dillard had gotten his gold medal anyway, despite the hurdle misfortunes. Later in the same Olympics, Dillard watched Porter win the hurdles in 13.9, not even close to his best time. But Dillard made up for his disappointment by picking up another gold medal when he ran the third leg of the relay and gave the Americans such a commanding lead they couldn't lose.

As for the Olympic hurdles, Dillard gave it another try four years later in Helsinki. In 1952, there would be no attempt at the 100 meters again; it would be the hurdles or bust. Harrison Dillard didn't bust. He made the team and won the Olympic final with a record-smashing 13.7 clocking.

1948 –1960 YACHTING
Paul Elvstrom Went from Novice to Master

The Danish entrant in the Firefly competition in yachting at the London Olympics had something to learn: he had never sailed one of the Fireflies before. Since sailing a Firefly is a one-man operation, he seemingly had a difficult task ahead.

That Paul Elvstrom, the 20-year-old novice, was at the Olympics at all was pure luck. Fortunately, the Games were being held in London, so it wasn't much cost for the Danish Olympic committee to send him. He had won the Danish trials for the Firefly class, but not in a Firefly itself. Neither he nor his fellow countrymen had one. Instead, Elvstrom qualified in a makeshift craft with a similar hull. When Elvstrom won in the trials, there was doubt that he would be sent to London. It took a coin flip by the committee to decide.

The Firefly competition would be graded on a complicated scoring system based upon seven races. Elvstrom was unfamiliar with the rules, new to international sailing, and shy. He withdrew from his first race by mistake.

His knowledge of sailing had been acquired by trial and error, going back to age 5 when his mother first let him alone in a boat which she kept attached to a dock with a towline. At 6, he was allowed to cast off. By 12, he had won a two-man championship against adults.

But that was all back in Denmark. At London, he was facing sailors who had gotten their ears wet in international regattas.

But Paul improved as he went along. In his second race at London he was sixth among the finishers. Then third, twelfth, and fifth, then first. With six of seven races completed, it was explained to him that he could actually win if he took the last race and the leader, an American, finished no better than fourth. Elvstrom won the race while the American came in fifth. Paul had his gold medal, much to the surprise of the seasoned opposition.

There wasn't any question about sending him to the next Olympics across the Baltic in Helsinki. And there wasn't any question about his winning. Sailing in what amounted to a version of the Finn class, Elvstrom won his first six races and wrapped up the gold. He sailed in the seventh race as a matter of dignity, and won that too.

He won the new Finn class in Melbourne in 1956 and thus set up the opportunity to become the first person to win an individual event at four consecutive Olympics. At Rome in 1960, he left little doubt that that was his objective. He had come out of temporary retirement at the request of the Danish Olympic committee. Just as he had eight years earlier, Elvstrom swept his first six races to clinch his record fourth gold. But he had to sit out the seventh race due to illness.

Edgy nerves and recurring headaches knocked Elvstrom out of competition for a while, and he was listed merely as a substitute for the 1964 Olympics. But by 1968, he had the wind in his sails again. At age 40 he almost won another medal.

It was then that *Sports Illustrated*'s water sports expert Coles Phinizy tried to explain what set Elvstrom apart from the other solo sailors: "He seems to use the wind and the water as if he owns them."

1948–1964 WATER POLO, 1952–1972 SWIMMING
The Gyarmatis Made the Olympics a Family Affair

There have been several cases of brother-brother, sister-sister, and husband-wife teams earning Olympic medals. Among them were the Press sisters from Russia in track and field, the Goitschel sisters of France in skiing, the Jenkins brothers of the United States in figure skating, Emil Zatopek and his wife Dana of Czechoslovakia in track and field, and so on. But how about this one:

Twenty-one-year-old Dezso Gyarmati of Hungary was a fine all-around water polo player who helped his country win a silver medal in the 1948 Games. And he kept starring for his country until he was 37. With Dezmo in the water, the Hungarians won the Olympic titles in 1952, 1956, and 1964 and finished thrid in 1960. But he wasn't the only one in the family bringing home the Olympic hardware.

Wife Eva won a gold medal under her maiden name Szekely for her performance in the 200-meter breaststroke

73

in 1952. Before the 1956 Games, their daughter Andrea was born (March 15, 1954), but Eva kept on competing and earned a silver medal in the same event in 1956.

It was only natural with a father who was a water polo star and a mother who was a swimming champion that Andrea would get into the swim of things, too.

But it was not "only natural" that Andrea would make such a big splash.

Andrea went to Mexico City for the 1968 Games when she was only 14. She turned in a creditable performance, finishing fifth in both the 100 backstroke and 100 butterfly.

Primed for another good showing at Munich in 1972, Andrea joined the family's list of medal winners. She took home a silver medal for her runner-up finish in the 100 backstroke and a bronze medal for the 100 butterfly.

1948–1956 BOXING
Laszlo Papp Didn't Beat around the Bushes

Laszlo Papp's goal in life was to become a professional boxer. But his country (Hungary) was a member of the Communist bloc after World War II, and it frowned on professional sports as being too capitalistic.

Papp's belief in himself was partly due to the Olympic middleweight championship he won in 1948, when he defeated Great Britain's John Wright. He dropped from the 161-pound class to a light middleweight ($156^1/_2$ pounds) for the 1952 Games and was just as powerful. He won again, this time defeating South Africa's Theunis van Schalkwyk for the gold medal. Only one other boxer had won two consecutive Olympic titles before.

Still, the Hungarian officials would not relent and allow Papp to turn pro. They preferred to have him capture gold medals for his country rather than earn real gold for himself.

In 1956, Papp turned in his finest performance. He defeated a Puerto Rican American, Jose Torres, for the light-middleweight title. Torres would go on to become light-heavyweight champion in the pro ranks and make a lot of money.

Papp was getting up in years then. When his best fighting days were behind him, the Hungarian government did a turnabout and let him try his luck against the professionals. But it was too late. Papp would have to be content with the fact that he was the only man to win three gold medals in Olympic boxing.

1952 FIGURE SKATING
Dick Button Executed a Triple Loop Jump

Figure skaters after World War II became much more sophisticated in their techniques and no one proved this better than a young American named Dick Button. A fast-rising star who became U.S. national men's singles champ at 16 and the international runner-up at 17, Button skated near flawlessly to win the 1948 Olympic title at age 18.

While becoming America's first gold medalist in figure skating, the graceful 5-foot 10-inch New Jerseyite gave the skating world a hint of things to come when he incorporated a 2½-revolution backward jump into his free-skating routine. It was something no one had done in competition before, and it was something so difficult that no one would match it by 1952, when the Winter Olympic stage moved to the outdoor rink at Oslo, Norway.

Button had easily outclassed the field in the 1948 Games at St. Moritz in the Swiss Alps. A world champion every year between the 1948 and 1952 Games, he was a strong favorite to repeat his Olympic victory.

But Dick, now a Harvard business student, was not content with merely winning. Naturally that was his goal, but he also wanted to perform a routine that would convince the skating world that he was giving them his best.

Button did exceptionally well in the compulsory figures that made up the first portion of the competition on the huge rink at Oslo. He held a commanding lead as the skaters later returned to the ice for the free skating—the most interesting part of the program.

He was now ready to treat the audience, which included some of the greatest experts and critics in skating, to a special surprise. For months, Dick had been working on a Triple Loop Jump. This took the $2^1/_2$-revolution jump a half-revolution further. Since no one had yet caught up to Dick's $2^1/_2$, it was a remarkable feat to try before such a critical audience.

The Triple Loop Jump is executed from the backward outside edge of the skate. Button, who perfected the maneuver by jumping off his right skate while going backward and then making three consecutive clockwise spins before landing, had only accomplished it to his full satisfaction about a half-dozen times in practice. He had never attempted it in competition before. But he had spent as much as six weeks concentrating on the maneuver.

Besides, his fear of failure was not that great even though a gold medal was at stake.

"I knew I was going to win with or without the Triple Loop Jump," he said. "But that wasn't my approach to competition. One has to exceed one's own level."

The free skating was held under the Norwegian moonlight at the lighted Olympic arena, and the ice conditions were good but not great as Dick began his 5-minute segment. Skating to the music from "Romanian Fantasy," he was a picture of perfection as he led up to the Triple Loop Jump with a series of flowing maneuvers. Then after about a minute and a half, he entered into the jump. Three times he spun as flawlessly as a gyroscope and landed smoothly on the back right side edge of his skate.

The reaction in the stands was that of awe, and total appreciation among those who knew the difficulty of what he had just done. Dick's reaction? "I was bloody well happy."

He didn't have time to gloat, however. In an unbroken sequence, he followed with a Triple Double Axle, another seemingly impossible feat, and three Double Axles, and later closed out the greatest free-skating routine the world had seen.

The Olympic judges gave him perfect 6-point scores, marking the first time that a skater had made a complete sweep. The gold medal was his again.

1952 TRACK AND FIELD
The Jamaicans Won a Relay Fair and Square

The United States rarely loses a relay race in the Olympic men's 400- or 1,600-meter events. And when the U.S. team does lose, there's usually a reason—a disqualification, dropped baton, or whatever.

The American quartets have won eleven of thirteen 400-meter (four runners each running 100 meters) races, and the only losses came on disqualifications. Likewise in the 1,600 there have been only four losses in thirteen Olympics, and a couple of those were on disqualifications when the United States was a strong favorite. But America did take an honest beating on one occasion—and it came from one of the most unlikely countries in the world. That was in 1952, when the U.S. 1,600-meter team, composed of an all-star cast, lost to Jamaica.

Jamaica is a small Caribbean nation that is smaller in both size and population than the state of Connecticut. Jamaicans love track and field, especially the sprint events. In the late 1940s and early 1950s, they developed some of the greatest quarter-milers ever assembled in such a small area.

First and foremost was Herb McKenley, one of the all-time greats in sprinting. Educated at the University of Illinois, he was one of the first foreign stars to make a name for himself at an American college. He set the world record in 440 yards at 46.2 in 1946, tied it a year later, then ran 46 flat in 1948, the year he finished second in the Olympics. He was a repeat runner-up in 1952, much to his disappointment because he was given the same time as the winner. He also was runner-up in the 100-meter sprint in the 1952 Games at Helsinki. Now, at age 30, he was making one last try for an Olympic gold medal, and it would have to come with the help of his teammates in the 1,600-meter relay.

But, oh, how he was expected to have help. One teammate, Gene Rhoden, had set the world record for the 400 meters in 1950 and beat McKenley out for the Olympic title in 1952 with a 45.9 clocking. Rhoden was a seasoned veteran who had little fear of the powerful U.S. team; as a college student at Morgan State in Maryland, he had won three National Collegiate Athletic Association titles in the 440-yard dash.

Another member of the Jamaican quartet was Arthur Wint, who won the 1948 Olympic 400 by nipping McKenley at the tape. Wint was fifth in the 400 in 1952 but earned additional laurels by taking the 800-meter gold medal. The final member of the foursome was Lester Laing, a more than able quarter-miler.

Their task was to beat a team from the United States—a nation with almost 100 times Jamaica's population and clearly the most powerful track and field country in the world.

The Americans boasted a pretty good all-star team of their own. Ollie Matson, who would later gain a name for himself in pro football, had finished third in the 1952 Olympic 400 in a time of 46.8 seconds. Gene Cole was a fine young runner out of Ohio. Charlie Moore was a former collegiate 440 champion (in 1949) and the current Olympic titlist in the 400-meter hurdles. Anchorman Mal Whitfield was America's all-time great half-miler and also a former bronze medalist in the 400 meters. Whitfield, who had just won his second Olympic 800, was the anchorman for the winning U.S. relay team that clobbered the field in 1948.

The race on the last day of the 1952 Games promised to be a close one, no matter who won. If something happened to the United States or Jamaica, there was always a powerful German team to push the survivor.

Wint led off against Matson. Laing, paired against Cole, allowed the American lead to stretch out to nearly 12 yards. Then came McKenley, the luckless Olympian, against gold medalist Moore.

Moore ran his heart out, going around the track in 46.2 seconds. The world record set by Rhoden was only 45.8. But McKenley began to eat up the track, looking for the elusive gold medal in his final year of running. His bony legs were lifted and put down in rapid fashion. He was out to run the race of his life—and he did. Herb covered the oval in an astounding time of 44.6 seconds, more than a second under the world record. When he gave the baton to Rhoden, he also gave him the lead.

Rhoden ran a strong race against the veteran Whitfield. As they neared the tape, it was anybody's gold medal. But Rhoden gave one last effort and nipped the American.

Jamaica's time was 3:03.9, a world record. The Americans, with nothing to be ashamed of, did 3:04.0. Most observers say it was the greatest relay race ever.

Americans, we said, have had more than their share of success in Olympic relays. But one American had more shares than anyone. He was Frank Wykoff, a former schoolboy sensation from California.

Only three runners have ever been members of more than one gold medal relay team—Loren Murchison (1920 and 1924 400-meter), Harrison Dillard (1948 and 1952 400-meter) and Wykoff. But what sets Wykoff apart from the others is that he was a member of three winning teams in the 400-meter baton race.

Wykoff was a member of the U.S. quartet that ran 41 seconds flat in 1928. A schoolboy then, he was put at the leadoff position. Four years later, he was moved to the crucial anchor position. A collegian at the time at Southern Cal, Wykoff brought the American team home in a world record 41 seconds flat. Then four years later, as a club athlete running in the Berlin Games with Jesse Owens, Wykoff was again the anchorman. And again a success. He protected the lead that Owens, the first runner, gave the team and sped home in 39.8 seconds, another world record. He retired not long after that.

1952 TRACK AND FIELD
Emil Zatopek's Triple Was Nearly Miraculous

Emil Zatopek's last name derives from a Czechoslovakian word meaning "to light a fire." The greatest distance runner of his time, and one of the truly greatest of all time, Zatopek ran like a man on fire. He was strange in appearance but a strongly built man who wore his races on his face. He would moan, groan, talk to other runners, laugh, complain, bite his tongue, and so on in varying degrees. "He ran like a man with a noose around his neck," said Red Smith, the famed sportswriter.

But if Zatopek's looks varied, his results didn't.

The Czech army officer assumed heavy assignments on the track but always came through—and usually in first place.

A runner before World War II, Zatopek's training regimen was impeded when fighting broke out. He picked up quickly after the war. He had not run the 10,000 before May of 1948 but emerged as the Olympic 10,000-meter champion and 5,000-meter runner-up. He was 25 years old.

By the time the Olympics moved to Helsinki, home of the great Finnish runners, in 1952, Zatopek was rated the supreme distance runner in the world.

Zatopek had his sights set high for Helsinki. He would try to become the first man to win both the 5,000 and 10,000 at the same Olympics since 1912, when a Finnish star completed the grueling double.

He won the 10,000 with little trouble, beating his own Olympic record by 42 seconds. He said he was disappointed, however, and that he would try to do better in the 5,000.

Two days after he won the 10,000, he had to compete in the 5,000 heats. Then, two days later would be the 5,000 final. Zatopek was unruffled by the thought of the schedule. He was pushed hard by a Frenchman and a German, but he still won and smashed the Olympic record by 11 seconds.

He had achieved something no runner had done in 40 years. Zatopek still was not satisfied. He said there was one more race he would attempt—the marathon, that 26-mile 385-yard test of man's durability and heart.

The race was scheduled for July 27, only eight days after Zatopek had opened his Olympic competition with the 10,000 victory.

Was such a triple possible?

In Zatopek's case, one could not take him too seriously if for no other reason than that he had never run a marathon in competition before!

But that did not dismay him. In fact, he was in a jovial mood as the horde of runners left the Helsinki stadium for the grueling race. Near the beginning, he said to an English marathoner, in English, "Excuse me, I have not run a marathon before but don't you think we ought to go faster?" With that, Zatopek took off and before long left the Englishman in the back of the pack with cramps.

Despite a field that included over five dozen seasoned marathoners, it was the amazing Czech who arrived back in the stadium first to collect yet another gold medal—and his most astounding one. He won by a minute and a half, and had enough energy left to run an enthusiastic victory lap to the delight of the fans. Later he would call the marathon "a boring race." The fans at Helsinki and amazed track experts from around the world could hardly agree in this case. They had just witnessed the climax of the greatest distance-running triple in history.

1952 BOXING
Floyd Patterson, at 17, Made a Step toward Fame

The United States had not won an Olympic boxing title in 20 years when Floyd Patterson ventured to Helsinki with the American team in 1952. Whether the Brooklyn youth could change that trend seemed to be a question boxing experts did not know how to handle.

Patterson was a shy youth, only 17 years old. Though no such records are kept, Olympic archivists could think of no one that young who had ever won a gold medal in boxing. But Patterson, a middleweight then (165 pounds), had fast fists and a general ring quickness that had some of those very same experts calling him a "young Sugar Ray Robinson." In 1952, a boxer could not get a higher compliment.

Patterson drew a bye on the first round, then displayed that quickness on July 29 when he won a very one-sided match against Omar Tebbaka of France, 3–0.

In his next outing, Patterson sent Leonardus Jansen of the Netherlands flying with a first-round kayo. Patterson got to him with a left hook to the point of the chin. It was the only punch he needed. Jansen went down and didn't twitch a muscle for over 10 seconds. "There hasn't been a KO like it in 200 bouts now," reported *The New York Times*.

A day later, Patterson won over Stig Sjolin of Sweden when the officials ruled that the Swede had held Floyd in the third round. The bout was more one-sided than it sounded. Patterson had blasted his opponent time and again with hooks, including occasional triple hooks, and had floored him three times. "Few professionals can throw hooks that fast and this youngster has the fight crowd here goggle-eyed," wrote the Associated Press's correspondent.

In the final, Patterson was pitted against Vasila Tita of Romania. Since Romania was part of the Communist bloc of nations, then involved in a cold war with the United States, and since the referee was from Poland, another Communist country, Patterson was warned by his handlers to be on guard.

Early in the bout, Patterson learned why the people in his corner were wary. When he spun around nowhere near his opponent, he was given a warning by the official. Then when Floyd finally caught the Romanian with an uppercut to the chin and sent him to the floor, the ref counted slowly. Even with that, Patterson had done such a good job that the foe stayed there, out for a good 20 seconds after the count began.

Floyd Patterson, age 17, had his gold medal.

1952–1956 DIVING
Pat McCormick Won a Double Double

The American success in Olympic diving goes back to the first competition in 1920. From then through the Munich Games in 1972, U.S. springboard and platform divers won 37 of a possible 48 gold medals, to say nothing of more than half the silver and bronze awards. But the U.S. divers have pretty much shared the wealth; only three men or women other than Pat McCormick have ever taken both the springboard and platform titles in the same Games, and only six other divers have won more than two first places.

But Pat McCormick was something special on the diving board—so special that in 1965 she became the first woman selected to the International *Swimming* Hall of Fame in Fort Lauderdale, Florida.

Born in Lakewood, California, Pat Keller became a championship diver in her native state. After she married airline pilot Glenn McCormick, she continued to compete. Her husband encouraged her to do so. Thus, in 1952, when she was 22, she earned an opportunity to go to Helsinki for the Olympic Games.

Pat was one of the older U.S. Olympians on the swimming and diving squad. America's traditional strength in diving (and swimming, too, for that matter) usually centered on its teenage prodigies. But Pat took both diving titles by substantial margins.

Mrs. McCormick continued to dominate U.S. diving up to 1956, another Olympic year. But she had to withdraw from active participation for much of the first half of 1956 while she was pregnant with her first child. She had five months to return to peak form before the 1956 Games at Melbourne late in the year.

With husband Glenn coaching her before and during the Olympics, Pat had no trouble defeating her teammate Jean Stunyo in the springboard event at the Olympics. But her chances for a second diving title seemed slim in the platform contest.

Going into her final dive, Pat was in fourth place, behind teammates and former medal winners Juno Irwin and Paula Jean Myers. She selected a potentially high-scoring but high-risk forward 1½ somersault with full twist as her last try for a medal. The odds were against her as she looked out from the 10-meter platform.

But her execution was excellent. Pat scored an 18.17 on her near-perfect dive to defeat Juno, 84.85 to 81.64. That gave her a fourth gold medal.

That also earned her the coveted Sullivan Award as the outstanding U.S. amateur athlete for 1956 and the Associated Press's Woman Athlete of the Year honors.

1956 TRACK AND FIELD
Hellsten and Ignatyev
Went to the Wire for a Medal

The running of the 400-meter dash at the 1956 Olympics figured to be close with a host of men capable of crossing the line in 47 seconds or less. But the judges couldn't believe just how close as four of them were bunched at the finish just three-tenths of a second apart. Never before had four men been separated by so little.

The time wasn't anything special, and America's Charley Jenkins, with a 46.7 clocking, was the clearcut winner. Karl Haas of Germany was second at 46.8. But the battle between Voitto Hellsten of Finland and Ardalion Ignatyev of the Soviet Union for third place—and the bronze medal—was so close, the judges finally gave up trying to decide who had crossed the line first. Both were clocked at 47 seconds flat. In an unprecedented, and unduplicated move, even though men with the same times have been separated before, the judges called it a dead heat. Both men received bronze medals.

Field events are easier to judge—all the officials have to do is get out the metric tape and measure. In fact, with sports becoming more and more sophisticated with each Olympics, splitting hairs has become even easier.

In the 1972 Games at Munich, West Germany, the organizers decided to utilize a highly sophisticated prismatic reflector system to measure the throws in the weight events. That turned out to be fine for a native West German named Klaus Wolfermann.

In its pre-Olympic forecasts, the authoritative *Track & Field News* stated, "The most erratic event [the javelin] has the surest bet of all in Jan Lusis." Going into the Games, the Russian spear thrower was so far ahead of the field that it seemed the only thing to do was *give* him the gold medal and let everyone else *compete* for the silver and the bronze.

But at Munich, Lusis at least found some competition in a late-blossoming physical education instructor from a nearby Bavarian town. Klaus Wolfermann was threatening to join Lusis, the defending Olympic champ and world record holder (307 feet 9 inches), in the 300-foot class.

Among the hammer, discus, shot, and javelin, the javelin goes for the longest distance. Ties are almost nonexistent, and 5- or 6-foot victories are not rare, even in high-caliber Olympic competition. Fortunately at Munich, the organizers used the impartial prismatic reflector system for there might have been claims of partiality and hometown decision.

Lusis led as expected after five throws with a 293-foot 9-inch toss. Then Wolfermann unleashed a heave of 296 feet 10 inches (or 90.48 meters, as it was recorded on the spot).

On his last throw, Lusis did 90.46 meters, or 296 feet $9^{1}/_{2}$ inches. A half inch, or 2 centimeters, separated the two—and that small margin spelled the difference between victory and defeat in the biggest upset of the Munich Games.

1956–1968 TRACK AND FIELD
Al Oerter Was Unbeatable in the Clutch

If Al Oerter stood out in any way among the leading discus-throwing aspirants at the 1956 Olympic Games, it was for his lack of credentials. Oerter was just 19 years old when he made the United States squad, and he was just a shade over 20 when he joined the field for the Olympic finals at Melbourne, Australia, in late November. His opposition, and the men expected to go 1-2-3 for the medals, were Adolfo Consolini of Italy, age 39; Fortune Gordien of the United States, age 34; and Ferenc Klics of Hungary, age 32. Each had been a veteran of two Olympics, and each had done well.

Furthermore the "big three" had distance as well as experience on the University of Kansas sophomore. Oerter's best throw had been 184 feet 2¾ inches, but that had been two years before with a high school discus. The Olympic platter was heavier and more difficult to throw. Besides, Gordien had thrown the regular discus 198 feet in a warmup toss, and Consolini had a pre-Olympic throw of 194.

In Olympic tuneup meets, Oerter had managed to reach 180 feet on several occasions, so he knew he at least had a chance at Melbourne despite the odds against him.

While Consolini, Klics, and Gordien got off mediocre first throws in the finale, Oerter concentrated his attention on a flag that marked the Olympic record (180 feet $6^{1}/_{2}$ inches away) and put all his nervous energy into his first throw. He hefted the discus 184 feet $10^{1}/_{2}$ inches, well over his previous best. The Olympic neophyte was in first place momentarily, much to his own surprise and that of the veterans. He also had the Olympic record temporarily.

Oerter continued to throw over 180 feet. Meanwhile, the others were having their problems. As it turned out, none even reached 180 feet though Gordien came close on his last toss and struck a little fear in Oerter. But Gordien could do no better than second, and another American, Desmond Koch, sneaked in for third. After the three Americans went to the victory stand to collect their medals, Oerter was still surprised. "I don't know how I ever did it," he said.

In the next four years, Oerter kept adding weight and muscle onto his 220-pound body, and he improved his style in an event that requires more technical skills than most track events. He added 10 feet to his best mark. But in the meantime, another threat entered the scene in the form of mammoth Richard (Rink) Babka, a fellow American who weighed almost 270 pounds and broke the 200-foot barrier in practice. Babka defeated Oerter in the U.S. Olympic trials, though Al easily made the team again.

At Rome, Oerter reached the 198-foot mark in practice just one day before the competition began. It was his best ever, and his confidence was buoyed. But Al could not get over 190 feet in his first four throws of the finals, while Babka maintained the lead with 190 feet 4 inches.

But on his last throw, Oerter came through with his best competitive toss when it counted most. His 194-foot 2-inch distance stole the gold medal out of Babka's grasp.

Oerter was now a two-time Olympic champion, though he had yet to set the world record. Between the 1960 Games at Rome and the 1964 Olympics at Tokyo, Oerter did manage to hold the world record by becoming the first man to throw over 200 feet in competition. But his reign was short-lived. Less than three weeks later, it was broken by a Russian.

Undismayed, Oerter boosted his weight to 250 pounds. A full-time employee of an electronics firm, Al had little time to work, raise his family, and train. But he had made up his mind that athletes in his event worked at sports too much anyway. He worked out by himself if and when he had the time. As the 1964 Games got closer, new threats emerged. One was Jay Silvester, an American, and another was Ludvik Danek, a Czech with a herculean 211-foot 9^1/$_2$-inch world record shortly before the Olympics. Oerter could not even win the American trials, losing to Silvester. Oerter's problems were multiplied by a neck injury that forced him to wear a brace.

When he got to Tokyo, Oerter's problems continued and he was all but counted out. Torn cartilages in his ribs made him quit training altogether for six days before the Games began. The U.S. team doctors suggested that he drop out, and he almost did.

Somehow, Al worked his way through the qualifying round, though, and was in the finals again. But Danek was living up to his favorite role with consistent throws over 190 feet, topped by a 198-foot 6^1/$_2$-inch Olympic record on his fourth throw. As Oerter plugged away, it seemed fruitless. Silvester and another American, Dave Weill, passed him by, and as his day went on, he got worse instead of better, dipping into the 178-foot class. Stiff with pain, he went into the circle for throw No. 5. With a burst of energy he still doesn't believe, Oerter unwound and sent the discus sailing. The scoreboard indicated 61 meters even, and Olympic veteran Oerter knew that meant over 200 feet—200 feet 1½ inches to be exact. The opposition couldn't come close on their final attempts, and Oerter again was a surprise champion.

Oerter now set his goal at winning a fourth gold medal, a feat no Olympian had ever achieved in discus throwing. The first leg of his preparation was a full year of rest. That gave him a healthy attitude, as well as a healthy body, when he returned to the circle in 1966 and lengthened his personal record to 207 feet 5 inches. But he went into a terrible slump the following season. Jay Silvester, with 218 feet 3½ inches, and several other discus throwers passed him by. Somehow, Oerter's competitive zeal earned him a place at the U.S. trials for the Games at Mexico City in 1968, but before he left for Mexico, Silvester boomed a throw over 224 feet and reached 230 on a foul. Al went to Mexico City as the sixth best discus thrower in 1968, almost 20 feet behind Silvester.

Oerter, now 32, was as clearcut an underdog as he had been 12 years before in his Olympic debut. "I didn't think I had a chance," he said.

At the Olympic workouts, Oerter decided to improve his mental outlook instead of trying to work on his technique. To do this, he would imagine himself throwing under all sorts of conditions and how he would adapt to being ahead or behind at any given point. When he went out to a rain-drenched track to compete, that strategy began to pay off. He threw better than his personal Olympic best on his initial toss, but Silvester had topped the Olympic record with 207 feet 9½ inches in the qualifying rounds. That was better than Al had done in or out of Olympic action.

After two throws in the finals, no one was exactly putting much distance between himself and Oerter. So Al reared back with the deepest concentration, spun, and sent the discus 212 feet 6½ inches, way over his best. When he almost matched that on his next-to-last and last throws, the opposition was completely psyched out. The pressure was just too much. Silvester began fouling, and Danek's attempts fell far short.

For a fourth and final time, Oerter had pulled an upset by throwing farther than ever when it counted most.

1956–1964 SWIMMING
Dawn Fraser Got Better As She Got Older

In a sport often monopolized by teenagers, Dawn Fraser was the speed queen of women's swimming until she was 27 years old. She ruled the most glamorous event, the 100-meter freestyle, for a decade and won three Olympic gold medals in that span. No other swimmer, male or female, has won golds at more than two Olympics.

But then no other swimmer could match the fun-loving Australian for staying power. Dawn's career began when she was 14 years old. With a high capacity for work, she was a world record holder and then Olympic champion three years later in 1956, when the Olympics were held in her native country. Dawn lowered her own world record in the 100 from 63.3 to 62 seconds in the Olympics.

She would continue to set world marks until she totaled 27 of them.

In the 100 alone, she broke the world mark four more times, lowering it to 60.2 seconds by 1960. That year, she won her second Olympic gold medal in the event, defeating

American champion Chris von Saltza by a full 3 yards in the short, fast race.

Dawn probably had 10,000 miles of training and competition behind her (according to her own estimate) before going to Tokyo in 1964 for her third Olympics. She was now 27 with a disdain for the tight discipline her country's officials imposed on their swimmers. Because she was supposed to compete on the first day after the opening ceremonies, she was told that she had to bypass the pageantry to preserve energy. She went anyway.

Apparently it didn't affect her swimming.

The field at Tokyo included a couple of American teenie-boppers, ages 15 and 16, who were supposed to be threats to Dawn's subminute record in the 100. In fact, in the final race one of them did dip below 60 seconds. But Dawn left that swimmer, Sharon Stouder, in the wake as she won yet another gold medal with a 59.5 clocking. Stouder did 59.9.

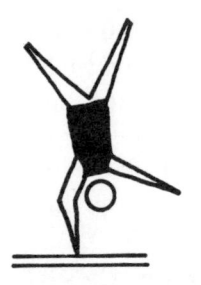

1956–1964 GYMNASTICS
Larisa Latynina Won a Record Number of Medals

The return of Russia to the Olympic Games in 1952 signaled young Larisa Latynina to begin preparing for the future. Gymnastics was her specialty, and it would be a sport the Soviets, who had been out of Olympic competition since 1912, would dominate—with her help.

Larisa got her first taste of Olympic competition in 1956, when she won a record four gold medals. She also won a silver and a bronze. It would be the best Olympic showing by the pretty Russian girl, but by far it would not be her last.

The Russian team was even better in 1960 at Rome, winning 15 out of a possible 16 women's medals. Larisa took her share—three golds, two silvers, and a bronze.

Larisa found her match for individual stardom in 1964, when a Czech, Vera Caslavska, won the all-around, horse vault, and balance beam. But Larisa kept Miss Caslavska from a complete sweep by defeating her in the floor exercises. It was Larisa's third straight gold medal in that event.

Larisa earned her third straight gold medal for her team's combined performance, too, and picked up two silver and two bronze medals.

That gave her a total of 18 medals, far more than anyone else had ever earned. And maybe more than anyone else will ever earn.

Year	Gold Medal	Silver Medal	Bronze Medal
1956	Individual combined Team combined Horse vault Floor exercises	Parallel bars	Team (portable apparatus)
1960	Individual combined Team combined Floor exercises	Balance beam Parallel bars	Horse vault
1964	Team combined Floor exercises	Individual combined Horse vault	Balance beam Parallel bars

1960 ICE HOCKEY
The Americans Benefited from Some Russian Detente

The idea of any sane odds maker giving the U.S. ice hockey team a chance to win the 1960 Olympic title was farfetched. While the Americans had always placed well in Olympic competition, winning medals in six of eight previous Winter Games, the possibility of even finishing in the top three in 1960 defied all odds. As for first place, hockey was a Canadian game—and virtually a monopoly.

The Canadians were coming in with one of their strongest teams, hoping for revenge against the 1956 champion Russian squad and surprise runner-up American sextet which had dented Canada's prestige. The Russians themselves, helped by the fact that their country did not have its best players in the pros as the Canadians did, were again strong. The Czechs and Swedes also were good and figured to be in the battle for the bronze medal.

The Americans, with eight players who had never skated in major international competition before, seemed like a ragtag team. There were five players left over from the 1956 squad which had upstaged the Canadians by sneaking in for the silver medal, but for the most part the 17-man group was made up of everyday citizens with no long-term hockey careers in their plans. There were carpenters, insurance men, a fireman, and a soldier among the group. The important goalie position was being manned by Jack McCartan, whose international experience included only two games, both of which the Americans had lost. He had originally been rejected by coach Jack Riley, but then was added to the team a week before the Olympics began at Squaw Valley, California.

The Americans opened up with a surprising victory over the Czechs and an easy win over the Australians to make it through the preliminary round.

In the championship round, the United States scored a 6–3 victory over the Swedes, as Roger Christian, an Olympic rookie, scored three goals, all of which were assisted by his brother Bill. The Cleary brothers, Bill and Bob, combined for five goals as the United States beat Germany in its next game, 9–1.

The Canadians, meanwhile, were beating their opponents in predictable fashion, by 12–0 and 4–0 scores. The American hopes for a medal picked up when the Swedes held the Russians to a 2–2 tie.

That left the United States with three final games in the round-robin playoffs. They would face the Canadians, Russians, and Czechs, in that order.

The battle against Canada was an Olympic classic. Bob Cleary scored midway through the first period as the United States hammered shots at the Canadian goalie. The trend was reversed in the second period as the Canadians attacked McCartan with 20 shots-on-goal. But McCartan covered the goal mouth brilliantly and turned them all away. Meanwhile, Paul Johnson, center on the U.S. team, scored to make it 2–0 by the end of the period. McCartan continued his outstanding play in the net in the final period as the Americans carefully guarded their lead. With $6^{1}/_{2}$ minutes to play, the Canadians scored, but McCartan's heroics—turning away 39 shots in the game—proved to be the difference in a 2–1 victory.

Next came the Russians, unbeaten but once tied.

A Soviet victory would vault the U.S.S.R. into first place and a virtual gold medal. And though the United States scored first on a goal by Bob Cleary, that seemed to be the best bet as the Russians stormed back with two goals of their own. McCartan was doing a good job in the nets but he needed help. Coach Jack Riley appealed to the team's pride between periods when he told them, "Everyone in the nation is counting on you guys. There are millions watching on television."

McCartan shut out the Russians in the final two periods, while Bob Christian was scoring two goals. The Americans had another stunning victory, 3–2, and would be going into their final games as odds-on favorites to win the gold medal. All they had to do was beat the Czechs again.

The Czechs weren't the pushovers the Americans expected, however. Taking advantage of the U.S. overconfidence and sluggishness, the Czechs commanded a 4–3 lead after two periods. Before the final period, the Americans got a surprise visitor in their dressing room. He was Nik Sologubov, the Russian team captain. The Soviets were destined for third place then, and possibly fourth if the Czechs won, so his advice wasn't hurting his own team when he suggested that the U.S. players try taking oxygen to perk up their listless bodies. It was a kind gesture considering that U.S.-Soviet political relations at the time were not much warmer than the ice on the rink.

The Americans heeded his advice. Revitalized, they bombarded the Czechs with six goals by the Cleary and Christian brothers, and wound up with a 9–4 victory. That clinched the gold medal and, at least for 17 U.S. hockey players, created some rare Russian-American détente.

1960 BASKETBALL
Jerry Lucas Had a Perfect Game

The 1960 United States basketball team was the most polished of all the great squads the Americans sent to the Olympics over the years. The deadly shooters that made up that squad connected on over 60 percent of their field goal attempts as a team, and combined they averaged 102 points a game, which is an unofficial Olympic record.

None of the U.S. players was a deadlier shooter at the Rome Olympics than Jerry Lucas, an Ohio State University undergraduate. In a game against the Japanese team on August 27, the 6-foot 7 1/4-inch Lucas shot 14 times from the floor. He made all 14, for what had to be the greatest display of marksmanship in Olympic history. For the entire 1960 Olympics, Lucas made over 70 percent of his field goal attempts.

No official records are kept of Olympic basketball, but some team and individual performances have stood out.

In the game in which Lucas made all those field goal attempts for a total of 28 points, the American team scored

125 points. That matched the 125 scored by China in its 125–25 drubbing of Iraq in the 1948 Games.

China's 100-point margin in the Iraq game set no record for the biggest point spread, however. The Korean team had beaten the Iraqis, 120–20, just a few nights before.

So much for offense. The defensive gem of the Olympics was a match at the 1936 Games in Germany. The Czechs beat the host German team 20–0.

Individual scoring feats are hard to dig out. But Radivoje Korac of Yugoslavia scored 192 points in eight games in the 1960 Olympics for an even 24-point average that may constitute the record. Individual game highs are even more difficult to dig out, but Russia's 6-foot 5-inch Otar Korkija scored 38 points in a 78–60 defeat of Chile in the 1952 Olympics.

1960 SWIMMING
Jeff Farrell's Guts Made Up for His Appendix

All seemed lost for pre-Olympic swimming favorite Jeff Farrell when he was stricken with an inflamed appendix just six days before the U.S. tryouts in early August 1960. Farrell, a 23-year-old Kansan and a Navy officer, had swum 100 meters freestyle in 54.8 seconds, fastest in the world. But that meant nothing for a possible three-gold winner when he went to the hospital for an emergency operation.

Farrell earned the admiration of his fellow swimmers at the Detroit trials when he got out of bed 24 hours after the operation and was back in the water training three days later. With his abdomen heavily taped, Farrell decided to make a bid for the team anyway.

He almost earned a chance to swim in the Olympic 100 when he churned through the water with great speed for 75 meters. Then he got too close to the ropes that divided the lanes, touched them, and lost valuable time. He missed second place, and a qualifying berth, by a mere one-tenth of a second. His 56.1 clocking was hardly close to his potential when healthy.

There was still one hope left for Farrell, though. A couple of days later, he'd try again, this time to make the 800-meter freestyle relay team by swimming in 200-meter trials. There, he would have to finish among the top six and hope that the coaches would choose him for the final quartet.

Farrell came in fourth, just a shade off the time posted by the runner-up. The U.S. coaching staff was now hoping he would recuperate fully in the next three weeks that remained before the Olympic competition in Rome. By qualifying for the team in the 800-meter relay, Farrell was now also eligible to be considered for anchorman of the Americans' 400-meter medley relay team, too. The last 100-meter leg of the medley required a freestyler.

At Rome, Farrell continued to mend. He was at poolside to watch Australian Jon Devitt and American Lance Larson battle each other in identical 55.2-second clockings in the 100-meter freestyle race, which was the race he had been pointing for until his appendectomy. But a few days later, on September 1 at Rome's Stadio del Nuoto, he would get his chance. His performances in training sessions at the Olympics had earned him the anchorman berths on both relays scheduled for that day.

Farrell moved so fast through the water in the 200-meter leg of the 800 relay that he helped the United States win. The team's clocking of 8:10.2 demolished both the Olympic (8:23.6) and world (8:16.6) records.

Then in the 400-meter medley relay, Farrell had a chance, unofficially, to match his speed with the 100-meter freestylers. After backstroker Frank McKinney, breaststroker Paul Hait, and butterflyer Lance Larson opened up a 7-meter lead for Farrell, Jeff knew he had only to coast the rest of the way to preserve a U.S. victory. He poured it on anyway.

Farrell's split was 54.9, better than the Olympic champ had done under more pressure. Farrell helped lower the U.S. team's time to 4:05.2, almost 7 seconds better than the runner-up Australian team and 5 seconds better than the world record.

Dick Roth, a 16-year-old Californian, wasn't suffering as badly as Farrell had, but he did have an appendicitis attack three days before his scheduled 400-meter individual medley at the 1964 Games at Tokyo. His chief opponent, a German named Gerhard Hetz, who had held the world record before Roth, had pneumonia on the day of the event.

But both Roth and Hetz were in the pool for the final.

In the race, Roth put up a good fight and took over the lead in the third—the breaststroke—segment of the four-stroke race. Then Hetz took over the lead in the freestyle leg wrap-up. But Roth, sore appendix and all, passed him by and won the gold medal. In world record time at that!

Hetz, despite his case of pneumonia, finished third. Roy Saari, another American who could only complain of a bad cold, finished second.

1960 TRACK AND FIELD
Otis Davis Came out of Nowhere to Win the 400

Otis Davis. The name becomes more obscure as time passes. He came out of nowhere in his midtwenties, flashed to a shocking Olympic victory and a world record when his country needed such a performance most, then drifted back into virtual obscurity again less than a year after his triumph.

Davis's emergence as an Olympic gold medal winner in the 1960 Games at Rome happened so fast, and under such bizarre circumstances, that his story was bound to be lost in time. But it is worth retelling.

Otis Davis was an itinerant basketball player of benchwarmer caliber at the University of Oregon in 1958 when the school's track coach, Bill Bowerman, wandered through the practice area one day. For some reason, the astute Bowerman—one of America's greatest coaches—liked what he saw. As he recalled later, "I 'discovered' Davis by watching him bound around like a kangaroo out there on the basketball court."

Davis was already 26 years old. The basketball team had the first option on him because he was given an athletic scholarship for that sport. Furthermore, Bowerman learned, Davis had never competed in track and field. Besides, 26 is an age when most Americans are giving up the sport instead of pursuing it.

Nevertheless, Bowerman asked Davis to give the sport a try after the basketball season.

Davis took the coach up on the offer. A springy 6-foot 1-inch athlete, Davis first tried out for the high jump but was a dismal failure. Then one day when the university's best sprinters were out of town to compete in a major relay meet, Otis was entered in the 100-yard dash against local athletes. He ran it in 9.8 seconds, an impressive debut considering his lack of experience and the nondescript opponents. Bowerman was impressed with that raw talent and worked hard to develop it. With less than six weeks' training, Davis won the 220-yard dash in the prestigious Pacific Coast Conference meet. The next season, as a college junior, he was switched to the quarter mile.

The 440 is a tougher race with more strategy involved. Despite little experience and an early-season injury that slowed his progress, Davis fared well. He won his conference's championship and was clocked at 46.2 seconds in another meet. But his lack of knowhow showed in the National Collegiate Athletic Association meet, where he qualified for the final but failed to finish among the top five.

As a college senior, Davis did not run for the university team because of a technicality involving his eligibility. But he worked out with the varsity and competed for a local club team. Davis continued to run fast quarter-mile races, but he lost as often as he won. A surprise victory in the 400 meters (the metric equivalent of the 440) at the National Amateur Athletic Union meet in June 1960 advanced him to the U.S. Olympic trials a week later.

Otis finished third in the trials, which was good enough to earn him a trip to Rome for the Olympics and also a probable place on the Americans' crack 1,600-meter relay quartet. Already he had performed a near miracle. Here was a 28-year-old, in his third year of track, with what Bowerman estimated was only about ten 440-yard or 400-meter races in his log, joining the powerful American squad for the Olympics.

To win at Rome—well, that would be asking for a real miracle.

The way the American men began falling at the 1970 Olympics, despite the premeet predictions, made Davis's task seem even more difficult. One after another, favored U.S. stars were beaten. The country's best sprinter, Ray Norton, was soundly whipped at both 100 and 200 meters. The United States failed to qualify any of its three men for the 800-meter final. America could do nothing in races over 800, either. The United States was being threatened with a shutout in the "flat" (nonhurdle) running events for the first time in its vaunted Olympic history.

Davis figured to have problems in the 400. If not from his teammates Jack Yerman and Earl Young, both of whom beat him in the trials, competition was expected from Carl Kaufmann of Germany and the Spence brothers from South Africa.

Yerman, however, had trouble in the heats, and Young had to struggle to make it to the final. Meanwhile, Davis kept pushing ahead. He proceeded to win his semifinal heat with an Olympic record time of 45.5. But he said, "I don't think I can go faster."

He did, though. In a grueling duel with Kaufmann and four others the next day, he matched the German stride for stride around the oval in unseasonably hot September weather. As they reached the tape, Kaufmann lunged for it while Davis sped through it. The crowd couldn't determine the winner until the official verdict was announced—Davis first, Kaufmann second. Their times were identical 44.9s, better than the world record. When Davis was asked about the comment he had made the day before, he said, "They *made* me go faster."

Later in the Olympics, Davis was at the anchor end of another world record. This time he clinched a U.S. victory in the 1,600-meter relay with a tremendous final 400 meters.

"I never dreamed I could do all this," he said. "I owe it all to Coach Bowerman." Then he promptly packed up his gold medals and sent them to the University of Oregon, where they were deposited in a vault for safe keeping.

Davis continued to run in a series of post-Olympic meets in Europe, but his results were hardly spectacular. The next season, at age 29, he ran rarely and closed out his career with a 440-yard victory in the National AAU meet.

1960–1964 TRACK AND FIELD
Abebe Bikila's "Footwork" Won Him Marathon Titles

When Abebe Bikila was a small boy growing up in Ethiopia, the fascist government in Italy overtook his homeland and held it through most of World War II. Because this was the only victory the fascist army could muster, poor little Ethiopia became the brunt of almost as many jokes as Mussolini's troops.

Though revenge wasn't his intention, Bikila conquered Rome in 1960 when he was 28 years old. It was ironic that the greatest triumph of his athletic career would come on Italian soil.

Abebe Bikila, all 128 pounds of him, seemed like just another competitor when he lined up with 68 other runners for the strength-sapping 26-mile 385-yard marathon at the 1960 Olympics. Many of those other contestants had bigger reputations as well as bigger bodies than the little private who was on leave from Emperor Haile Selassie's corps of bodyguards. Bikila had run a marathon in 2 hours 21 minutes and 23 seconds in the past, but the critics figured that the Ethiopian trails that he ran on were not as well saturated with officials as the route in Rome would be. What made Bikila's so-called good time suspect was that he could do no better than third in his own country's Olympic trials; that wasn't very good in a country not known for quality distance runners.

The critics had one more laugh when Abebe lined up for the race at Rome: he wasn't even wearing shoes. The race was scheduled to be run in part over the cobblestone Appian Way, the historic road built and traveled by the legions of the Roman Empire. Compared with any modern highway, that was expected to be misery for even the well-heeled marathoners from Europe, Asia, and North America. As for a barefooted man, no way.

As Bikila made his way over the closely watched course, his biggest problem became the mobs of crowds cheering him on. His own countrymen were darting out on the route to offer him water, which he spurned. And at one point, he was almost run over by a motorcycle.

He managed to break away from the cheering pack the way he had broken away from his fellow marathoners, and he strutted back into Stadio Olimpico a full 25 seconds ahead of the second-place man. Bikila's time of 2 hours 15 minutes and 16.2 seconds was a full 8 minutes better than the great Emil Zatopek had done eight years before.

Records aren't official in the marathon because the courses vary so much. But Bikila's time—the best in Olympic history—and his victory made believers of all those who snickered at his shoeless tactics.

Upon returning to Ethiopia, Bikila was promoted to sergeant in the palace guard. As his nation's first Olympic champion, he was treated like royalty.

He didn't let the royal treatment get the best of him, though, as he prepared for a defense of his laurel at Tokyo in 1964. Repeating an Olympic marathon victory is a much tougher feat than winning the first time. No one had ever done it. In fact, few runners had ever tried.

Between Olympics, Bikila gave little indication that he could do it. He ran in the world-famous Boston Marathon in 1963, and though he led for some of the race, he finished a mediocre fifth. His Ethiopian running mate, Mamo Wolde, was looking more and more like the man to beat in Tokyo.

At the starting line in the 1964 Games, Bikila toed the mark wearing shoes. He wasn't about to take any chances. He moved fast through the streets of Tokyo, grabbing the lead and stretching it out. When he reached the stadium for the final traditional laps around the track to conclude his victory, his foes were not even in sight. His victory margin was over 4 minutes—the widest margin between first and second places in four decades of Olympic competition. His time was a remarkable 2 hours 12 minutes 11.2 seconds, better than any man had ever done over the standard marathon distance.

Bikila acknowledged the crowd, then went to the middle of the infield where he began a series of exercises that drove the fans into a frenzy.

Upon his return to Ethiopia, he again was promoted. This time he was made a lieutenant.

Abebe was among the athletes who gathered for the running of yet another Olympic marathon in Mexico City in 1968. But his age (36), the pressures of publicity, and his physical condition were working against him. A small fracture in his foot became very painful, and he dropped out of the race after covering a third of the distance. "If this had been my first marathon," he said later, "I would have gone on. But I have already won two gold medals and the pain was too great to bear." His friend, Mamo Wolde, held up the Ethiopian tradition by winning, though his time hardly compared with Bikila's great mark in 1964. Still, it was a moral victory for Abebe, who had put his nation on the athletic map.

Abebe went home intending to keep on competing. But in March of 1969 he was involved in a near-fatal automobile crash. His legs were paralyzed.

Bikila made it to the 1972 Olympics in Munich, though. Traveling around the Olympic Village in a wheelchair, he was an honored guest of the West German government and just as popular as ever. Two years later, he died.

1964 SPEED SKATING
Lidija Skoblikova Was a Paavo Nurmi on Ice

The introduction of women's speed skating to the Winter Olympics at Squaw Valley, California, in 1960 also introduced the sports world to a bright blond-haired Russian girl named Lidija Skoblikova. The 20-year-old physiology student managed to accomplish what only a couple of women athletes in any sport had ever done in the Winter Olympics before—win two gold medals. Her victories in 1,500 and 3,000 meters, plus a fourth-place finish in the 1,000, made her one of the most versatile female skaters ever.

Lidija was still in top form, and expected to be better than ever for the longer speed-skating events, when she arrived at the 1964 Games at Innsbruck, Austria. Given a bit of the luck that speed skaters need, she was a favorite to take three events this time—the 1,000, 1,500, and 3,000. That would, if achieved, match the performances of two Norwegian men (Ivar Ballangrud, 1936, and Hjalmar Anderson, 1952) who had each taken three golds in a single Olympics.

The women's events in the 1964 Games opened with the 500, which is as different from the 3,000 meters as a 100-yard dash in track is from a half-mile run. Lidija was entered, though.

As competition began, she watched her Soviet teammate Irina Egorova flash across the ice in 45.4 seconds to break the Olympic record. Then a second Russian teammate almost matched that time as the next set of sprinters took to the ice. Lidija just pushed all the harder on her turn and raced home a winner in 45 seconds flat—almost a second under the former Olympic best. It was considered somewhat of an upset for a skater better attuned to the longer distances.

The possibility now loomed that Lidija could sweep all four events, and win four golds. The only other woman to ever win as many as three golds in Winter Olympic competition was Sonja Henie, the Norwegian figure skater, and it took her 12 years to do it. Lidija could match that in four days.

But Lidija expressed concern for her Russian teammates, who had figured to dominate the speed-skating events. They were off to a good start with a 1-2-3 finish in the first event as Lidija wondered aloud if she were being too greedy at the expense of her friends, and even reportedly wept over the thought.

Her concern was alleviated, however, when her husband sent her a congratulatory telegram from the U.S.S.R. and told her, in effect, "Go for broke—win them all."

The next day, she won the 1,500 and broke another Olympic record—her own. The following day, she won the 1,000, again in record time.

With the toughest race, but her best one, coming up, she was all set to try for the grand slam. The fourth race presented a different problem for her. The ice at Innsbruck was beginning to soften, and the draw for positions had a dozen skaters, racing in twosomes, going out ahead of her. The more skaters on the ice, the worse the softening effect becomes. And soft ice naturally slows down skaters, whose medals are determined by comparative times.

As Lidija pumped her skates into the ice at a rate of about two steps for every second, her chances seemed to wane. At about the halfway point, she heard her time, and it didn't sound very good. When she speeded up, her advisers alongside the course suggested that she slow down to avoid a spill. But Lidija wasn't about to be content with just another medal—she wanted the fourth gold.

She finished the race in 5 minutes 14.9 seconds, which wasn't as good as her own Olympic record. But it was good enough for first place in 1964, and that was good enough for her.

1964 SKIING
The Goitschel Sisters
Go 1-2 ... and 2-1

Alpine skiing, naturally, is identified with the Alps—those towering mountains that draw together Austria, Germany, Italy, and France. But the French had little to cheer about going into the 1964 Winter Olympics at Innsbruck, Austria, in those Alps. The Frenchwomen, as good as they were on the slopes, had not earned a medal of any sort—gold, silver, or bronze—since women's Alpine events were inaugurated in 1952.

Several years before the 1964 Games, two French sisters from the Alpine community of Val d'Isere dropped out of school and decided to take up skiing full-time. In the early 1960s, Marielle and Christine Goitschel developed into two of the finest Alpine skiers their country had ever known.

Strangely enough, though they skied together throughout their lives, they developed completely different styles. Christine, quieter though by no reason shy, became an elegant skier who took a race course apart like a surgeon. Younger Marielle attacked it like a butcher, not afraid to bull her way through the flags that make up the course.

The contrasting styles didn't bother either sister's development, however. As 1964 neared, it was obvious both would be in the running for Olympic medals and were good bets—along with America's Jean Saubert—to win the golds in the two slalom contests.

In the first of the events, Christine masterfully held her poise on her runs down the slalom, aiming meticulously for the spots she wanted to hit without being thrown off by the gates. Marielle, in swashbuckling fashion, barreled by the gates, not worrying about being detoured slightly if she hit one or two. Christine's graceful style won out—and won her a gold medal. But Marielle was close behind in second place. Saubert, the favorite, was third.

It was a great day for the French, and no one typified it better than President Charles De Gaulle, who dashed off a telegram: "I wish you to know, mesdemoiselles, that the whole people are very proud of your victory."

But the sisters were not finished. Two days later, the giant slalom was scheduled on a wide-open course with few difficult curves. It was a course made for Marielle and Jean Saubert.

This time the gold went, not surprisingly, to Marielle, and it marked the first time sisters had won during the same Olympics. But Christine slipped in for a second place, giving the Goitchels 1-2 in both races—a feat that will be even tougher to match.

If the Goitchels were proud to have two gold medals in the family, so were two brothers who preceded them in Winter Olympic competition.

The 1956 Olympic men's figure-skating crown went to Hayes Alan Jenkins, who led a 1-2-3 American sweep in the event. The third-place finisher that year, though hardly in the class with Hayes, was his brother David.

Four years later, however, after Hayes retired from the amateur ranks, David came through at Squaw Valley, California, with a solid victory that retained the gold medal for the United States—and for the Jenkins family.

1964 TRACK AND FIELD
Billy Mills Shocked Everybody but Himself

The least talked-about American runner at the 1964 Olympics was Billy Mills—until after his race. Not one reporter bothered to ask him a question, much less get a prerace interview. But that was somewhat understandable. Americans had never done well in the 10,000-meter run, and Mills's credentials just weren't that good. His best times weren't even close to those posted by world record holder Ron Clarke of Australia or any of several other runners. Mills's best 10,000 time was 55 seconds slower than Clarke's.

But the 26-year-old Mills, who was also scheduled for the marathon run, had been training so well he figured he had a chance even if no one else thought so.

As the 38 runners took off, Mills tried to stay with the leaders. That was his plan of attack: stay up front as long as he could. Halfway through the race, Mills found himself leading the pack of five runners who still had a reasonable chance. Then the race settled down to Mills, Clarke, and a strong-running Mohamed Gammoudi of Tunisia. Mills and Clarke fought for the lead on the last lap, but Gammoudi rushed up fast. In doing so, he bumped Mills accidently and threw him off stride. Mills fell 8 yards behind. It turned out to work in his favor, though, as the outside of the track was harder and easier to sprint on. Mills raced up to the front runners with 50 meters left. Then he raced past them to pull one of the most stunning upsets in Olympic history.

Mills won in 28:24.4, a full 46 seconds better than he had done in the past. It was an Olympic record.

Afterward, Clarke, who finished third, was asked if he had included Mills in his prerace plan. "I never heard of him before," the veteran Australian had to admit.

1964 VOLLEYBALL
Japan's Women Treated Defeat Like Death

Masae Kasai, the 30-year-old captain of a spinning mill factory team that represented Japan in women's volleyball, had a simple credo in leading her squad: "We have never experienced defeat; we must win."

Winning was something that came often to the Kaizuka Amazons. But it didn't come easy. They paid for their many victories with bloodied fingers, floor-burned bodies, some broken bones and dislocated joints, and overall sacrifices that would make normal hard-working athletes look like sissies.

The 16-woman squad certainly had no room for sissies. The team's driving coach, Hirofumi Diamatsu, saw to that. The girls went through a daily schedule that read like this: up at 7 in the morning, to the factory for full-time jobs from 8 to 3:30, and to practice at 4. The team worked out until midnight six days a week. On the seventh day, Sunday, they didn't rest—they practiced all day! That was the schedule

51 weeks a year, for several years. There was no time for marriage, family, or fun.

The team was carefully selected from the factory workers. There were no extra benefits for the athletes, whose average salaries were about $50 a month. They practiced in an unheated gymnasium and were asked—told—to go through grueling drills.

The regimen paid dividends, though. By the time the team ventured to Tokyo for the first Olympic volleyball tournament for women, it boasted a winning streak of well over 100 for more than four years. One of those victories had been in the 1963 world championship game, and it marked the first in many years that a country outside the Communist bloc of nations had won that title.

The Japanese were not expected to win many gold medals even though they were hosting the 1964 Olympic Games, so naturally the country looked up to the factory team girls. They were something to look up to—the girls averaged 5 feet 7 inches, taller than most Japanese men.

At Tokyo, everyone else was looking up to them, too.

Not surprisingly, Japan and the Soviet Union battled their way to the showdown.

The Japanese girls won the first set 15–11, with the six starters sipping tea later while the crowd went wild. The next two sets were closer, but with the same result—Japan winning. And with three sets, they won the game and the gold medal.

For the first time in years, there was a chance to relax.

The girls became such national heroines that their victory was not forgotten after the Games were concluded. When it was pointed out that they had had no time to meet men during their several years of training, the Emperor himself stepped in and asked the nation to help find husbands for the girls. They had no problem meeting men after that.

1968 TRACK AND FIELD
Bob Beamon Jumped for Joy High above Sea Level

World records aren't exactly a dime a dozen, but they do get broken with regularity in Olympic Games if for no other reason than that the quadrennial contests provide the athletes with their greatest competition. The athletes who gathered at Mexico City in 1968 knew that, but they also knew that the 1½-mile-high altitude was going to play havoc with some events. In track and field, the jumpers and short-distance runners were supposed to benefit the most, for the higher one goes above sea level, the thinner the air is. That in turn makes for less resistance.

Bob Beamon, a storklike American long jumper, had all the facts on file as he prepared for the Olympic finals. He had easily made the U.S. team with a wind-aided jump of 27 feet 6½ inches—the longest ever but not a record because of the wind factor. Beamon did hold the indoor record at 27 feet 1 inch. And outdoors he twice upped his personal bests legally—first to 27 feet 2³/₄ inches and then to 27 feet 4 inches—in pre-Olympic meets in 1968.

Though he was the youngest jumper in the field at age 22, and despite the fact that he would be matched against three of the greatest jumpers of all time, he was the favorite to win in Mexico City. Most experts felt that he, or whoever won, would have to jump 28 feet. Competition and altitude would force the athletes to break the 28-foot barrier for the first time.

The 1968 long-jump field was clearly the greatest ever. Along with Beamon there was Ralph Boston, the 1960 gold medalist and 1964 runner-up; Igor Ter-Ovanesyan, an Olympic veteran who shared the world record of 27 feet 4³/₄ inches with Boston; and Lynn Davies, the man who upset Boston at Tokyo in 1964. Boston was an American, Ter-Ovanesyan a Russian, and Davies a Britisher.

Despite the formidable field, Beamon remained the favorite. A 6-foot 5-inch high jumper and a 9.5-second sprinter, he had all the tools to lift his lanky frame over 28 feet. Competitively, he brought a string of 22 straight victories with him to Mexico City.

Beamon may have been feeling the pressures as competition got underway. He nearly fouled out in the qualifying round as he kept missing his steps. One of those fouled jumps was for 27 feet 6 inches, further than the world record, and a foot further than the existing Olympic record. But with the foul, it was merely a piece of trivia for the track and field buffs.

Altogether, Beamon fouled twice and scratched twice. He had one last jump in which to qualify for the finals. So he shortened his stride to choppy steps and landed safely at 26 feet 10¹/₂ inches. That advanced him to the finals.

Beamon decided that his way of avoiding the pressure in the finals would be to make his best effort on his initial jump—and let the others resolve the psychological problem if he was successful. The other three, meanwhile, were already toying with Beamon's unlimited potential in their minds. "I'm always nervous when Beamon goes down the runway," said Boston, "because you know that some day he's going to put all that great talent together in one big jump."

There were 17 jumpers in the finals on a mid-October day, and three of them were jumping before Beamon. With the temperature cooling, making the artificial runway harder and confusing to figure out, Beamon watched all three foul. Beamon took that into consideration as he roared down the track for his first leap. He hit the board perfectly without breaking stride, and lifted himself like a bird. A slight but legal 2-meters-per-second breeze helped carry his 6-foot 3-inch, 165-pound body through the air. When he landed, he jumped for joy, knowing he had done well.

An official notified him that his leap was 8.90 meters. Bob knew that 8.60 meters equaled 28 feet 2 3/4 inches, which was his goal, so he was even more excited. Someone quickly converted the 8.90 for him; it equaled an astounding 29 feet 2 1/2 inches—16 inches over the world record!

Beamon went into a daze and kissed the earth he had leaped over. "Tell me I'm not dreaming," he asked of anyone who approached him. The track buffs figured that a 29-foot 2 1/2 inch jump was comparable to a 3:43.3 mile or a 7-foot 10 1/2-inch high jump, two statistics that had not even come close to being approached.

Beamon's initial jump was enough for victory. The other jumpers wilted under the strain of thinking about it. Davies could jump only 21 feet 1 3/4 inches on his next try. Boston just shook his head in awe.

Cordner Nelson, editor of *Track & Field News* and an observer of many track feats while covering six Olympics, wrote later that Beamon had given "probably the greatest single performance in the history of the sport."

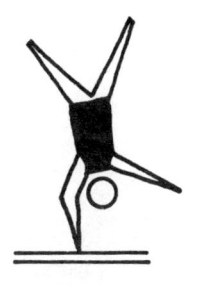

1972 GYMNASTICS
Olga Korbut Bent over Backward for Her Fans

In the official report of the XXth Olympiad, it was pointed out that "for the future someone will have to invent a gymnastics hall to seat 100,000 spectators so that 50 percent of those desiring to see the events will have an opportunity. There seems to be no end in sight to the number of persons desiring to see women's gymnastics." A lot of the hoopla over women's gymnastics at those 1972 Games in Munich centered on a pig-tailed Russian teen-ager named Olga Korbut.

For those who like to analyze such statements, there may have been a question whether Olga Korbut promoted the status of gymnastics or vice versa. Whatever the case, the petite 4-foot 10-inch Soviet girl won for herself more avid followers than any other female athlete in recent memory.

If the 12,000-seat Sporthalle at Munich was not a large enough stage for Olga, it has been estimated that on one night of Olympic gymnastics competition alone some 800 million people from 78 nations watched her perform via television. What they saw caused many viewers to fall in love with her, a fact brought out by many journalists covering the events. When she was asked about this suddenly developed rapport with the fans, she replied: "Maybe they love me because they know I love them very much."

Olga, at age 17, may not have been the best all-around gymnast at the Munich Games. In fact, her teammate Ludmilla Turischeva probably was. Yet Olga—younger, smaller (at 84 pounds), and more personable—had a stronger hold on the crowd.

But Olga was not without real talent.

A gymnast since the age of 9, she moved fast through the ranks of Soviet gymnastics. That is not easy; the Russian women have won 58 of the 90 gold medals in Olympic competition. By the time she was 15, Olga was allowed to compete in the U.S.S.R. national championships even though there was a minimum-age rule (16) that had to be waived. It was at that national meet that she first displayed the backward somersault on the balance beam that astounded—and confused—the officials. They didn't know how to score it because they hadn't seen it before. The next year, she earned a place on the Soviet's international team. She was awarded her country's coveted "Master of Sport" title at an earlier age than any other gymnast.

Olga's best performances were on the balance beam, on the uneven parallel bars, and in the floor exercises—almost in that order. By 1972, she and Miss Turischeva were regarded as two of the finest gymnasts in the world.

But at Munich, Olga's magnetic personality sometimes overshadowed her true sports ability.

On the first day of competition, in the combined exercises, Olga stunned the crowd at Sporthalle and a worldwide television audience with a backward somersault on the beam. It was a feat unprecedented by man or woman in Olympic history and would not be duplicated by anyone but Olga at Munich. If the movement was not familiar to gymnastics fans, it was to Olga. Though an original accomplishment that no one else had ever matched as far as anyone knew, Olga often did it as many as 100 times a day in practice sessions.

The crowd cheered her as she daringly flipped backward and landed safely on the four-inch-wide beam at Munich. "In a moment, Olga Korbut became Olga," said one journalist trying to capture the audience's reaction to the unique leap.

She also successfully performed her other original feat—nicknamed a "flik flak"—on the uneven parallel bars. The flik flak is her term for a brave half-backward somersault in which she swings around the top bar and comes down to catch the lower bar with her hands in the middle of her exercise. No one else has ever dared to try it in competition. No one but Olga.

Her stunning feats not only won her the crowd but also her first gold medal.

Two nights later, she stubbed her toe while participating in the individual competition in the uneven parallel bars and tumbled to the floor before she could complete a flik flak. Her routine was spoiled, and it cost her heavily in the scoring. As she sadly walked to the corner, she was in tears. She sat, head bowed, knowing the slipup had cost her a gold medal. But her sadness managed to draw the sympathy of the fans into her corner, too.

The next night, when the finals of the individual events were held, she regained her poise. She finished with a silver medal in the uneven parallel bars, then performed another backward somersault on the beam that helped gain her a gold medal. She ended her Olympic competition with a somewhat surprising victory in the floor exercises. By then, the crowd was so solidly behind her that it probably would not have allowed the judges to escape had they not named her the victor.

How good were her backward somersaults and flik flaks?

A year after the Olympics ended, the international gymnastics federation tried to ban them. What the rules makers were suggesting was that the feats were impossible, or at least too dangerous for the athletes to try. Olga disagreed. Perhaps for others, but not for her. "It has always been considered that gymnasts have the right to determine their own style," she said. When she threatened to retire if the ban was imposed, the international body reconsidered.

Olga had scored another stunning victory, even if she was not given a gold medal for it.

1972 WRESTLING
Ivan Yarygin Pinned Defeat on Opponents

Ivan Yarygin wasn't supposed to win the heavyweight freestyle wrestling gold medal at Munich. A fellow Russian, Shasta Lomidze, the 1971 world champion, was. But Yarygin filled in for his teammate once the Games got underway, and there were no regrets by the people in his corner. The 23-year-old Yarygin quickly pinned his first opponent in the 220-pound class. He got the second and third men on pins, too, and just as quickly. Before ending up on the winner's stand with a gold medal, Yarygin pinned seven men in seven matches in a total elapsed time of 18 minutes 8 seconds. (A single match, if carried to the end, is made up of three 3-minute periods.)

The man Yarygin replaced as heavyweight champion was Russian teammate Alexander Medved. Medved had some wrestling honors of his own—and he wasn't done collecting them when he reached Munich on the same plane with Yarygin.

The 34-year-old teacher had won the light-heavyweight title at Tokyo in 1964 and the heavyweight crown in 1968. Then in 1972, he moved up to the newly established super-heavyweight class, a group of bruisers that included a 420-pound American, Chris Taylor.

Medved disposed of Taylor and other super heavyweights bigger than himself to take his third gold medal in as many Olympics. Considering that he never weighed in over 250 pounds, it was a super, super windup of his career.

1972 TRACK AND FIELD
Kip Keino's Form
Was Strictly Championship

There were a lot of people, including his own Kenyan Olympic committee, who didn't think Kipchoge Keino should be running the 3,000-meter steeplechase at the 1972 Olympics. Kip was expected to win the more prestigious 1,500 race later on in the Olympics, just as he had in remarkable fashion in Mexico City in 1968.

Kip was expected to be anything but remarkable in the steeplechase, where an inexperienced runner can smack up his legs on the hurdles or twist an ankle after slipping in a water hazard. And inexperienced Kip was.

The 1972 season was the first year Kip took the steeplechase seriously. And not too seriously at that. Before the September running of the event at Munich, Kip had only four international races in the event. He had won a couple of local races in Kenya, but even then he had lost three times and had never won in matches with countryman Ben Jipcho.

Worldwide, 30 athletes had better times than his best going into the Olympics. About two dozen of those runners were on hand for the race at Munich. Keino's 8:30.0 clocking looked paltry compared with the 8:22s to 8:24s which had been run and which were expected to be duplicated by some of the top Europeans at Munich.

It wasn't that Kip couldn't run. After all, he was the top-rated 1,500 man and one of the best 5,000 men of all time. The 3,000-meter distance of the steeplechase was sandwiched nicely in the middle of those other lengths. But the steeplechase course is made up of several hurdles, some with water hazards in front of them. At 5 feet 10 inches Kip seemed just a little too short for the hurdling, and at 32 years old he seemed definitely too old to be taking up a new event.

But Kip ran anyway.

He ran second in his qualifying heat to Tapio Kantanen, a Finn who was one of the favorites. Keino's time of 8:27.6 was better than he had ever done. But that time was nothing compared with the Olympic record 8:23.8 set by another countryman, Amos Biwott, in another heat. Regardless, Keino advanced to the finals, which were saturated with Finns and Kenyans.

The final started slowly, which helped Keino, who was stepping up on the hurdles instead of gliding over them. That's time-consuming. Kip stayed with the pack and was fourth after 2,000 meters. That was fine with him because he did not want to be bunched with the front runners in case somebody fell or knocked him down going over a hurdle.

In the last couple of laps. Keino moved up. And with one to go, it was he and Ben Jipcho out in front. Kantanen moved up as Keino slowed at yet another hurdle. But in the stretch run it was all Keino. He won by a full second in 8:23.6, Olympic record time.

A week later, Keino lost the 1,500, so in retrospect his decision to run the steeplechase was a wise one.

1972 TRACK AND FIELD
Lasse Viren "Rose" to the Occasion

Finland seemed to have a likely prospect in its quest to regain its long-lost prestige in distance running, but 1972 appeared to be somewhat premature for Lasse Viren to accomplish this. For all his raw talent, the lanky, 23-year-old Viren just didn't appear to have the experience necessary for victory when he toed the starting line of the 10,000-meter run at the 1972 Olympics at Munich.

Viren had run the 10,000, which is about $6^1/_4$ miles, less than ten times, and with mixed results. Viren had tied the Finnish national record and had the best time among the Olympic hopefuls, but he also had a smattering of defeats among his distance races in the Olympic year. His teammate Juha Vaatainen, plus East German Jurgen Hasse and Great Britain's Dave Bedford, were rated better. Besides, the 10,000 is one of those races that is a free-for-all.

But Viren went to the starting line with as much hope and confidence as anyone that September third, two days after qualifying fourth in his heat. His pre-Olympic talk was that he was going to Munich to break Bedford's European record and possibly undercut Australian Ron Clarke's world mark of 27 minutes 39.4 seconds. The youthful shaggy hair and thin beard on his boyish face was almost a sign of defiance to the more seasoned runners.

Viren lost no time getting into the footrace. He stayed with the front runners despite a stepped-up pace that had everyone threatening Clarke's world record. But the pace proved to be ridiculous and had some runners doing strange things.

On the twelfth of 25 laps around the crowded Munich stadium, Viren was bunched with several other men trying to keep up with Bedford's grueling tactics. As several flag-waving Finnish nationals in the stands put their faith in Viren, who was their hope after Vaatainen was forced to withdraw due to injury, Lasse ran too closely behind Belgium's Emil Puttemans. Viren put a hand forward to avoid a spill, but this only slowed him down and he backed into the runner behind him. That threw Lasse completely off stride, and he stumbled to the brown artificial track. As Viren skidded to a halt, grinding his shoulder into the track, another contender, Mohamed Gammoudi of Tunisia, ran over him and also was grounded.

In the stands, the flapping Finnish banners also came to a halt. It looked as though the Finns would have to pin their hopes on other distance races for 1972. Viren was down for at least three full seconds, and the pack of runners gained about 10 meters on him as he tried to regain his composure. Gammoudi, a former Olympic medalist, lay on the track ahead of him—a beaten, pathetic sight. But Lasse, his youthful enthusiasm lifting him to his feet again, sped after the field of runners.

No foul was called, so he was safe there. But seven runners had gained valuable ground midway through the race. His right thigh was sore from being run over, and he feared momentarily that he might burn himself out if he pushed himself too fast to catch up, but Viren sprinted to rejoin the pack.

Bedford led the runners past the 6,000-meter mark in a time close to Clarke's world record pace. Then Viren, bolstered by a crowd of 80,000 that cheered his courage, took the lead.

At 8,000 meters, there were only five runners left—and one of the most poised, surprisingly, was Lasse. Viren jockeyed for the lead with other runners until the final lap; then, upon hearing the bell, began pulling away as if he were on the final leg of a 4-minute mile. Lasse outsprinted Puttemans to the tape, doing the lap in 56.4 seconds.

Viren, who had picked himself off the ground after a seemingly sure defeat, was the Olympic champ. And not just in Olympic record time, either. His 27:38.4 clocking broke the world record. The flag-waving Finns stormed out of the stands to lead him in a victory lap, and it's safe to say that some of their pulses were beating faster than his, despite his remarkable race. The physiologists noted that Lasse's heart was pumping at a rate of merely 120, extremely low for such a pulsating performance.

No 10,000-meter victory in the Olympics, even under such unusual conditions, is a fluke. But a week later, Viren erased any doubts to that effect by adding the Olympic 5,000-meter gold medal to his collection.

Those triumphs, along with teammate Pekka Vasala's stunning upset in the 1,500 meters, had again turned the finish line into the "Finnish Line," as it had been in the days of Paavo Nurmi.

1972 SWIMMING
Mark Spitz Was the Greatest Goldfish of Them All

The scene at the 1968 Olympic Games at Mexico City was not a good one for Mark Spitz, a teen-aged Californian who was supposed to dominate the swimming program. Underneath the stands, three American girls who had just finished 1-2-3 in an event were being interviewed while Spitz was finishing up a race. When the race was over, one of the girls asked how Mark had done. When a reporter said last, the girls looked at one another and smiled. Mark Spitz, the arrogant and boastful would-be superstar, had failed again.

By most people's standards, Spitz's two gold medals, one silver, and one bronze would have been considered a fine showing. But more was expected of Spitz, who went to Mexico City touted—and sometimes touting himself—as the greatest short-distance freestyler and butterflyer the world had ever known. His only golds at Mexico were the result of swimming on the Americans' unbeatable relay teams. The silver and bronze medals came in individual events. That medal haul was far short of the six golds Spitz and a lot of other people predicted.

At Mexico, Spitz was a victim of tonsillitis, diarrhea, and the jitters as well as his own inflated prediction. Between then and the 1972 Games at Munich, there was a lot of growing up to do.

To Spitz's credit, he did it.

As a 22-year-old Indiana University graduate, Spitz was a much more tolerable human being at Munich. Some of the same people who had once cheered against him were now in his corner.

He was again given a big task—seven gold medals were openly being predicted by sportswriters and sportscasters, as well as other experts. But Spitz was better able to handle the pressure.

"It's been a lot of hard work since Mexico City," he would say. "A lot of times I wondered if I would do the same thing as in Mexico."

But he did not. In his first time in the Munich waters once the Games began, Mark splashed to an Olympic record in a 200-meter butterfly heat. That same day, he won the butterfly final in world record time and swam a brilliant anchor leg in the 400 freestyle relay to collect another gold.

The rest of Spitz's story is pretty well known. He went on to set an Olympic record by collecting seven golds in seven attempts at Munich, and signed a million-dollar contract after the Games were over to parlay those seven golds into more negotiable gold.

Mark's personal coach, Sharm Chavoor, probably summed it up best after the seventh gold medal was won, when he said: "He did a pretty good job for a guy who was supposed to choke."

In all, Spitz had brought his medal total to nine golds, one silver, and one bronze. When he retired after the last race in Munich, he was credited with 13 world records, not counting those he shared with relay teammates.

MARK SPITZ'S OLYMPIC LOG—1972

Event	Result	Comment
August 28		
200 butterfly heat	1st, 2:02.11	Olympic record
200 butterfly final	1st, 2:00.70	World record
400 freestyle relay	1st, 3:26.42*	World record; swam 50.90 anchor leg; did not swim in heats
August 29		
200 freestyle heat	1st, 1:55.29	Best time by anyone; close to Olympic record
200 freestyle final	1st, 1:52.78	World record
August 30		
100 butterfly heat	1st, 56.45	Tied for best time in heats
100 butterfly semifinal	1st, 55.98	Best time of anyone; just shy of Olympic record
August 31		
800 freestyle relay	1st, 7:35.78*	World record; swam 1:54.24 anchor leg; did not swim in heats
100 butterfly final	1st, 54.27	World record
September 2		
100 freestyle heat	2d, 52.46	3d fastest time overall; close to Olympic record
100 freestyle semifinal	2d, 52.43	
September 3		
100 freestyle final	1st, 51.22	World record; 0.43 ahead of runner-up time
September 4		
400 medley relay	1st, 7:35.78*	World record; swam 54.78 butterfly (third) leg; did not swim in heats

*Denotes team's time, not Spitz's.

1972 SWIMMING
Shane Gould Logged Her Share of Time in Water, Too

If Mark Spitz's 13 trips up and down the Olympic pool sounds like a heavy load, consider what 15-year-old Shane Gould did in the women's events of the 1972 Olympics.

The 5-foot 7-inch, 132-pound Australian girl had a tough assignment facing legions of fresh American swimmers day after day. But Shane held her own. She was in the water 12 different times, more than any other female swimmer had ever attempted. She came out of the water with three gold medals, one silver, and one bronze—all in individual events where she had to carry the load by herself. In her only relay attempt, her teammates were hopelessly outclassed by the time she swam the anchor leg, so her effort there was wasted.

Shane not only swam almost as many times as Spitz did, but she also swam in longer events.

She swam, and placed, in all four of the women's

freestyle contests—the 100, 200, 400, and 800. She was third in the 100 (and just 0.04 of a second behind the runner-up), first in the 200 in world record time, first in the 400 in world record time, and second in the 800. Her other success came in the 200-meter individual medley, where she won the gold medal in world record time. That had been her first event after qualifying sixth out of eight.

Shane's dozen different swims included heats, semifinals, five finals, and one relay final.

GOLD MEDAL WINNERS
SUMMER OLYMPICS 1896–1972

ARCHERY

MEN
1972—John Williams, U.S.A.

WOMEN
1972—Doreen Wilber, U.S.A.

**ATHLETICS—MEN
(Track and Field)
100 METERS**

	Sec.
1896—Thomas Burke, U.S.A.	12.0
1900—Francis Jarvis, U.S.A.	10.8
1904—Archie Hahn, U.S.A.	11.0
1908—Reginald Walker, So. Africa	10.8
1912—Ralph Craig, U.S.A.	10.8
1920—Charles Paddock, U.S.A.	10.8
1924—Harold Abrahams, Gt. Britain	10.6
1928—Percy Williams, Canada	10.8
1932—Eddie Tolan, U.S.A.	10.3
1936—Jesse Owens, U.S.A.	10.3
1948—Harrison Dillard, U.S.A.	10.3
1952—Lindy Remigino, U.S.A.	10.4
1956—Bobby Morrow, U.S.A.	10.5
1960—Armin Hary, Germany	10.2
1964—Robert Hayes, U.S.A.	10.0
1968—Jim Hines, U.S.A.	9.9*
1972—Valery Borzov, U.S.S.R.	10.1

200 METERS

	Sec.
1900—J. W. Tewksbury, U.S.A.	22.2
1904—Archie Hahn, U.S.A.	21.6
1908—Robert Kerr, Canada	22.6
1912—Ralph Craig, U.S.A.	21.7
1920—Allan Woodring, U.S.A.	22.0
1924—Jackson Scholz, U.S.A.	21.6
1928—Percy Williams, Canada	21.8
1932—Eddie Tolan, U.S.A.	21.2
1936—Jesse Owens, U.S.A.	20.7
1948—Mel Patton, U.S.A.	21.1
1952—Andrew Stanfield, U.S.A.	20.7
1956—Bobby Morrow, U.S.A.	20.6

*Indicates Olympic record

400 METERS

	Sec.
1896—Thomas Burke, U.S.A.	54.2
1900—Maxwell Long, U.S.A.	49.4
1904—Harry Hillman, U.S.A.	49.2
1908—Wyndham Hallswelle, Gt. Britain	50.0
1912—Charles Reidpath, U.S.A.	48.2
1920—Bevil Rudd, South Africa	49.6
1924—Eric Liddel, Gt. Britain	47.6
1928—Ray Barbuti, U.S.A.	47.8
1932—William Carr, U.S.A.	46.2
1936—Archie Williams, U.S.A.	46.5
1948—Arthur Wint, Jamaica	46.2
1952—George Rhoden, Jamaica	45.9
1956—Charles Jenkins, U.S.A.	46.7
1960—Otis Davis, U.S.A.	44.9
1964—Michael Larrabee, U.S.A.	45.1
1968—Lee Evans, U.S.A.	43.8*
1972—Vince Matthews, U.S.A.	44.7

100 METERS (continued)

	Sec.
1960—Livio Berruti, Italy	20.5
1964—Henry Carr, U.S.A.	20.3
1968—Tommie Smith, U.S.A.	19.8*
1972—Valery Borzov, U.S.S.R.	20.0

800 METERS

	Min.-Sec.
1896—Edwin Flack, Australia	2:11.0
1900—Alfred Tysoe, Gt. Britain	2:01.4
1904—James Lightbody, U.S.A.	1:56.0
1908—Mel Sheppard, U.S.A.	1:52.8
1912—James Meredith, U.S.A.	1:51.9
1920—Alfred Hill, Gt. Britain	1:53.4
1924—Douglas Lowe, Gt. Britain	1:52.4
1928—Douglas Lowe, Gt. Britain	1:51.8
1932—Thomas Hampson, Gt. Britain	1:49.8
1936—John Woodruff, U.S.A.	1:52.9
1948—Mal Whitfield, U.S.A.	1:49.2
1952—Mal Whitfield, U.S.A.	1:49.2
1956—Thomas Courtney, U.S.A.	1:47.7
1960—Peter Snell, New Zealand	1:46.3
1964—Peter Snell, New Zealand	1:45.1
1968—Ralph Doubell, Australia	1:44.3*
1972—Dave Wottle, U.S.A.	1:45.9

1,500 METERS

	Min.-Sec.
1896—Edwin Flack, Australia	4:33.2
1900—Charles Bennett, Gt. Britain	4:06.2
1904—James Lightbody, U.S.A.	4:05.4
1908—Mel Sheppard, U.S.A.	4:03.4
1912—Arnold Strode-Jackson, Gt. Britain	3:56.8
1920—Albert Hill, Gt. Britain	4:01.8
1924—Paavo Nurmi, Finland	3:53.6
1928—Harri Larva, Finland	3:53.2
1932—Luigi Beccali, Italy	3:51.2
1936—Jack Lovelock, New Zealand	3:47.8
1948—Henry Eriksson, Sweden	3:49.8
1952—Joseph Barthel, Luxembourg	3:45.2
1956—Ronald Delany, Ireland	3:41.2
1960—Herbert Elliott, Australia	3:35.6
1964—Peter Snell, New Zealand	3:38.1
1968—Kip Keino, Kenya	3:34.9*
1972—Pekka Vasala, Finland	3:36.3

5,000 METERS

	Min.-Sec.
1912—Hannes Kolehmainen, Finland	14:36.6
1920—Joseph Guillemot, France	14:55.6
1924—Paavo Nurmi, Finland	14:31.2
1928—Ville Ritola, Finland	14:38.0
1932—Lauri Lehtinen, Finland	14:30.0
1936—Gunnar Hockert, Finland	14:22.2
1948—Gaston Reiff, Belgium	14:17.6
1952—Emil Zatopek, Czech.	14:06.6
1956—Vladimir Kuts, U.S.S.R.	13:39.6
1960—Murray Halberg, N. Zealand	13:43.4
1964—Robert K. Schul, U.S.A.	13:48.8
1968—M. Gammoudi, Tunisia	14:05.0
1972—Lasse Viren, Finland	13:26.4*

10,000 METERS

	Min.-Sec.
1912—H. Kolehmainen, Finland	31:20.8
1920—Paavo Nurmi, Finland	31:45.8
1924—Ville Ritola, Finland	30:23.2
1928—Paavo Nurmi, Finland	30:18.8
1932—Janusz Kusocinski, Poland	30:11.4
1936—Ilmari Salminen, Finland	30:15.4
1948—Emil Zatopek, Czech.	29:59.6
1952—Emil Zatopek, Czech.	29:17.0
1956—Vladimir Kuts, U.S.S.R.	28:45.6
1960—Pyotr Bolotnikov, U.S.S.R.	28:32.2
1964—William Mills, U.S.A.	28:24.4
1968—N. Temu, Kenya	29:27.4
1972—Lasse Viren, Finland	27:38.4*

*Indicates Olympic record

Gold Medal Winners Summer Olympics 1892–1972 / 149

MARATHON

	Hr.-Min.-Sec.
1896—Spiridon Loues, Greece	2:58.50.0
1900—Michel Theato, France	2:59.45.0
1904—Thomas Hicks, U.S.A.	3:28.53.0
1908—John Hayes, U.S.A.	2:55:18.4
1912—Ken McArthur, So. Africa	2:36:54.8
1920—H. Kolehmainen, Finland	2:32:35.8
1924—Albin Stenroos, Finland	2:41:22.6
1928—A. B. El Ouafi, France	2:32:57.0
1932—Juan Zabala, Argentina	2:31:36.0
1936—Kitei Son, Japan	2:29:19.2
1948—Delfo Cabrera, Argentina	2:34:51.6
1952—Emil Zatopek, Czech.	2:23:03.2
1956—Alain Mimoun, France	2:25:00.0
1960—Abebe Bikila, Ethiopia	2:15:16.2
1964—Abebe Bikila, Ethiopia	2:12:11.2*
1968—M. Wolde, Ethiopia	2:20:26.4
1972—Frank Shorter, U.S.A.	2:12:19.8

20-KILOMETER WALK

	Hr.-Min.-Sec.
1956—Leonid Spirine, U.S.S.R.	1:31:27.4
1960—V. Golubnichy, U.S.S.R.	1:34:07.2
1964—Ken Matthews, Gt. Britain	1:29:34.0
1968—V. Golubnichy, U.S.S.R.	1:33:58.4
1972—Peter Frenkel, E. Germany	1:26:42.4*

50-KILOMETER WALK

	Hr.-Min.-Sec.
1932—Thomas Green, Gt. Britain	4:50:10.0
1936—Harold Whitlock, Gt. Britain	4:30:41.4
1948—John Ljunggreen, Sweden	4:41:52.0
1952—Giuseppe Dordoni, Italy	4:28:07.8
1956—Norman Read, N. Zealand	4:30:42.8
1960—Donald Thompson, Gt. Britain	4:25:30.0
1964—Abon Pamich, Italy	4:11:12.4
1968—C. Hohne, E. Germany	4:20:13.6
1972—B. Kannenberg, W. Germany	3:56:11.6*

110-METER HURDLES

1896—Thomas Curtis, U.S.A.	17.6†
1900—Alvin Kraenzlein, U.S.A.	15.4
1904—Fred Schule, U.S.A.	16.0
1908—Forrest Smithson, U.S.A.	15.0
1912—Fred Kelley, U.S.A.	15.1
1920—Earl Thompson, Canada	14.8
1924—Daniel Kinsey, U.S.A.	15.0

*Indicates Olympic record

1928—Sydney Atkinson, South Africa	14.8
1932—George Saling, U.S.A.	14.6
1936—Forrest Towns, U.S.A.	14.2
1948—William Porter, U.S.A.	13.9
1952—Harrison Dillard, U.S.A.	13.7
1956—Lee Calhoun, U.S.A.	13.5
1960—Lee Calhoun, U.S.A.	13.8
1964—Hayes Jones, U.S.A.	13.6
1968—Willie Davenport, U.S.A.	13.3
1972—Rod Milburn, U.S.A.	13.2*

†100 meters.

400-METER HURDLES

	Sec.
1900—J. W. Tewksbury, U.S.A.	57.6
1904—Harry Hillman, U.S.A.	53.0
1908—Charles Bacon, U.S.A.	55.0
1912—Not on program	
1920—Frank Loomis, U.S.A.	54.0
1924—Morgan Taylor, U.S.A.	52.6
1928—David Burghley, Gt. Britain	53.4
1932—Robert Tisdall, Ireland	51.8
1936—Glenn Hardin, U.S.A.	52.4
1948—Roy Cochran, U.S.A.	51.1
1952—Charles Moore, U.S.A.	50.8
1956—Glenn Davis, U.S.A.	50.1
1960—Glenn Davis, U.S.A.	49.3
1964—Warren Cawley, U.S.A.	49.6
1968—Dave Hemery, Gt. Britain	48.1
1972—John Akii-Bua, Uganda	47.8*

3,000-METER STEEPLECHASE

	Min.-Sec.
1920—Percy Hodge, Gt. Britain	10:00.4
1924—Ville Ritola, Finland	9:33.6
1928—Toivo Loukola, Finland	9:21.8
1932—Volmari Iso-Hollo, Finland	10:33.4†
1936—Volmari Iso-Hollo, Finland	9:03.8
1948—Thore Sjostrand, Sweden	9:04.6
1952—Horace Ashenfelter, U.S.A.	8:45.4
1956—Chris Brasher, Gt. Britain	8:41.2
1960—Z. Kryszkowiak, Poland	8:34.2
1964—Gaston Roelants, Belgium	8:30.8
1968—Amos Biwott, Kenya	8:51.0
1972—Kip Keino, Kenya	8:23.6*

†3,460 meters—ran extra lap in error by officials.

4 × 100-METER RELAY

	Sec.
1912—Great Britain	42.4

150 / Incredible Olympic Feats

1920—United States	42.2
1924—United States	41.0
1928—United States	41.0
1932—United States	40.0
1936—United States	39.8
1948—United States	40.6
1952—United States	40.1
1956—United States	39.5
1960—Germany	39.5
1964—United States	39.0
1968—United States	38.2*
1972—United States	38.2*

4 × 400-METER RELAY

	Min.-Sec
1908—United States	3:29.4
1912—United States	3:16.6
1920—Great Britain	3:22.2
1924—United States	3:16.0
1928—United States	3:14.2
1932—United States	3:08.2
1936—Great Britain	3:09.0
1948—United States	3:10.4
1952—Jamaica	3:03.9
1956—United States	3:04.8
1960—United States	3:02.2
1964—United States	3:00.7
1968—United States	2:56.1*
1972—Kenya	2:59.8

LONG JUMP

1896—Ellery Clark, U.S.A.	20'	10"
1900—Alvin Kraenzlein, U.S.A.	23'	6⅞"
1904—Myer Prinstein, U.S.A.	24'	1"
1908—Francis Irons, U.S.A.	24'	6½"
1912—Albert Gutterson, U.S.A.	24'	11¼"
1920—W. Pettersson, Sweden	23'	5½"
1924—DeHart Hubbard, U.S.A.	24'	5⅛"
1928—Edward Hamm, U.S.A.	25'	4¾"
1932—Edward Gordon, U.S.A.	25'	¾"
1936—Jesse Owens, U.S.A.	26'	5⅜"
1948—Willie Steele, U.S.A.	25'	8"
1952—Jerome Biffle, U.S.A.	24'	10"
1956—Gregory Bell, U.S.A.	25'	8¼"
1960—Ralph Boston, U.S.A.	26'	7¾"
1964—Lynn Davies, Gt. Britain	26'	5¾"
1968—Bob Beamon, U.S.A.	29'	2½"*
1972—Randy Williams, U.S.A.	27'	½"

*Indicates Olympic record

TRIPLE JUMP

1896—James Connolly, U.S.A.	45'	0"
1900—Myer Prinstein, U.S.A.	47'	4¼"
1904—Myer Prinstein, U.S.A.	47'	0"
1908—Timothy Ahearne, Gt. Britain	48'	11¼"
1912—Gustaf Lindblom, Sweden	48'	5⅛"
1920—Villho Tuulos, Finland	47'	6⅞"
1924—Archibald Winter, Australia	50'	11⅛"
1928—Mikio Oda, Japan	49'	10¹³⁄₁₆"
1932—Chuhei Nambu, Japan	51'	7"
1936—Naoto Tajima, Japan	52'	5⅞"
1948—Arne Ahman, Sweden	50'	6¼"
1952—Adhemar Ferreira da Silva, Brazil	53'	2½"
1956—A. da Silva, Brazil	53'	7½"
1960—Jozef Schmidt, Poland	55'	1¾"
1964—Jozef Schmidt, Poland	55'	3¼"
1968—Victor Sanev, U.S.S.R.	57'	¾"*
1972—Victor Sanev, U.S.S.R.	56'	11"

HIGH JUMP

1896—Ellery Clark, U.S.A.	5'	11¼"
1900—Irving Baxter, U.S.A.	6'	2⅘"
1904—Samuel Jones, U.S.A.	5'	11"
1908—Harry Porter, U.S.A.	6'	3"
1912—Alma Richards, U.S.A.	6'	4"
1920—Richmond Landon, U.S.A.	6'	4¼"
1924—Harold Osborn, U.S.A.	6'	5¹⁵⁄₁₆"
1928—Robert King, U.S.A.	6'	4⅜"
1932—Duncan McNaughton, Canada	6'	5⅝"
1936—Cornelius Johnson, U.S.A.	6'	7¹⁵⁄₁₆"
1948—John Winter, Australia	6'	6"
1952—Walter Davis, U.S.A.	6'	8¼"
1956—Charles Dumas, U.S.A.	6'	11¼"
1960—Robert Shavlakadze, U.S.S.R.	7'	1"
1964—Valery Brumel, U.S.S.R.	7'	1¾"
1968—Dick Fosbury, U.S.A.	7'	4¼"*
1972—Yuri Tarmak, U.S.S.R.	7'	3¾"

POLE VAULT

1896—William Hoyt, U.S.A.	10'	9¾"
1900—Irving Baxter, U.S.A.	10'	9⁹⁄₁₀"
1904—Charles Dvorak, U.S.A.	11'	6"
1908—Albert Gilbert and Edward Cook, Jr., both U.S.A.	12'	2"

Gold Medal Winners Summer Olympics 1892–1972 / *151*

1912—Harry Babcock, U.S.A.	12' 11½"	1960—Al Oerter, U.S.A.	194' 2"
1920—Frank Foss, U.S.A.	12' 5 9/16"	1964—Al Oerter, U.S.A.	200' 1½"
1924—Lee Barnes, U.S.A.	12' 11½"	1968—Al Oerter, U.S.A.	212' 6"*
1928—Sabin Carr. U.S.A.	13' 9⅜"	1972—Ludvig Danek, Czech.	211' 3"
1932—William Miller, U.S.A.	14' 1⅞"		
1936—Earle Meadows, U.S.A.	14' 3¼"		
1948—Guinn Smith, U.S.A.	14' 1¼"	**JAVELIN THROW**	
1952—Robert Richards, U.S.A.	14' 11¼"	1908—Erik Lemming, Sweden	178' 7½"
1956—Robert Richards, U.S.A.	14' 11½"	1912—Erik Lemming, Sweden	198' 11¼"
1960—Donald Bragg, U.S.A.	15' 5⅛"	1920—Jonni Myrra, Finland	215' 9¾"
1964—Fred Hansen, U.S.A.	16' 8¾"	1924—Jonni Myrra, Finland	206' 6¾"
1968—Bob Seagren, U.S.A.	17' 8½"	1928—Erik Lundquist, Sweden	218' 6⅛"
1972—Wolfgang Nordwig, E. Ger.	18' ½"*	1932—Matti Jarvinen, Finland	238' 7"
		1936—Gerhard Stock, Germany	235' 8 5/16"
		1948—Tapio Kaj Rautavaara, Finland	228' 10½"
SHOT PUT		1952—Cy Young, U.S.A.	242' 0¾"
1896—Robert Garrett, U.S.A.	36' 9¾"	1956—Egil Danielson, Norway	281' 2¼"
1900—Richard Sheldon, U.S.A.	46' 3⅛"	1960—Viktor Tsibulenko, U.S.S.R.	277' 8⅜"
1904—Ralph Rose, U.S.A.	48' 7"	1964—Pauli Nevala, Finland	271' 2¼"
1908—Ralph Rose, U.S.A.	46' 7½"	1968—Jan Lusis, U.S.S.R.	295' 7"
1912—Pat McDonald, U.S.A.	50' 4"	1972—Klaus Wolferman, W. Ger.	296' 10"*
1920—Ville Porhola, Finland	48' 7⅛"		
1924—Clarence Houser, U.S.A.	49' 2½"		
1928—John Kuck, U.S.A.	52' 0 13/16"	**HAMMER THROW**	
1932—Leo Sexton, U.S.A.	52' 5 15/16"	1900—John Flanagan, U.S.A.	167' 4"
1936—Hans Woellke, Germany	53' 1¾"	1904—John Flanagan, U.S.A.	168' 1"
1948—Wilbur Thompson, U.S.A.	56' 2"	1908—John Flanagan, U.S.A.	170' 4¼"
1952—Parry O'Brien, Jr., U.S.A.	57' 1½"	1912—Matt McGrath, U.S.A.	179' 7⅛"
1956—Parry O'Brien, Jr., U.S.A.	60' 11"	1920—Patrick Ryan, U.S.A.	173' 5⅝"
1960—William Nieder, U.S.A.	64' 6¾"	1924—Fred Tootell, U.S.A.	174' 10¼"
1964—Dallas Long, U.S.A.	66' 8¼"	1928—Patrick O'Callaghan, Ireland	168' 7½"
1968—Randy Matson, U.S.A.	67' 4¾"	1932—P. O'Callaghan, Ireland	176' 10 13/16"
1972—Wladyslaw Komar, Poland	69' 6"*	1936—Karl Hein, Germany	185' 4"
		1948—Imre Nemeth, Hungary	183' 11½"
		1952—Jozsef Csermak, Hungary	197' 11 9/16"
DISCUS THROW		1956—Harold Connolly, U.S.A.	207' 3½"
1896—Robert Garrett, U.S.A.	95' 7½"	1960—Vasiliy Rudenkov, U.S.S.R.	220' 1⅝"
1900—Rudolf Bauer, Hungary	118' 2 9/10"	1964—Romuald Klim, U.S.S.R.	228' 9½"
1904—Martin Sheridan, U.S.A.	128' 10½"	1968—G. Zsivotzky, U.S.S.R.	240' 8"
1908—Martin Sheridan, U.S.A.	134' 2"	1972—Anatoli Bondarchuk, U.S.S.R.	248' 8"*
1912—Armas Taipale, Finland	145' 0 9/16"		
1920—Elmer Niklander, Finland	146' 7"		
1924—Clarence Houser, U.S.A.	151' 5¼"		
1928—C. Houser, U.S.A.	155' 3"		
1932—John Anderson, U.S.A.	162' 4 7/16"	**DECATHLON†**	
1936—Ken Carpenter, U.S.A.	165' 7½"	1912—Hugo Wieslander, Sweden	
1948—Adolofo Consolini, Italy	173' 2"	1920—Helga Lovland, Norway	
1952—Sim Iness, U.S.A.	180' 6½"	1924—Harold Osborn, U.S.A.	
1956—Al Oerter, U.S.A.	184' 10½"	1928—Paavo Yrjola, Finland	

*Indicates Olympic record

1932—James Bausch, U.S.A.
1936—Glenn Morris, U.S.A.
1948—Robert Mathias, U.S.A.
1952—Robert Mathias, U.S.A.
1956—Milton Campbell, U.S.A.
1960—Rafer Johnson, U.S.A.
1964—Willi Holdorf, Germany
1968—Bill Toomey, U.S.A.
1972—Nikolai Avilov, U.S.S.R.
†Based upon point system which is updated from time to time.

800 METERS

	Min.-Sec.
1928—Lina Radke Batschauer, Germany	2:16.8
1960—Ludmila Lysenko-Shevcova, U.S.S.R.	2:04.3
1964—Ann Packer, Great Britain	2:01.1
1968—Madeline Manning, U.S.A.	2:00.9
1972—Hildegard Falck, W. Germany	1:58.6*

1,500 METERS

1972—Ludmilla Bragina, U.S.S.R.	4:01.4*

ATHLETICS—WOMEN
(Track and Field)
100 METERS

	Sec.
1928—Elizabeth Robinson, U.S.A.	12.2
1932—Stella Walasiewicz, Poland	11.9
1936—Helen Stephens, U.S.A.	11.5
1948—Francina Blankers-Koen, Netherlands	11.9
1952—Marjorie Jackson, Australia	11.5
1956—Betty Cuthbert, Australia	11.5
1960—Wilma Rudolph, U.S.A.	11.0†
1964—Wyomia Tyus, U.S.A.	11.4
1968—Wyomia Tyus, U.S.A.	11.0*
1972—Renate Stecher, E. Germany	11.0*

†Wind-aided; no record

4 × 100-METER RELAY

1928—Canada	48.4
1932—United States	47.0
1936—United States	46.9
1948—Netherlands	47.5
1952—United States	45.9
1956—Australia	44.5
1960—United States	44.5
1964—Poland	43.6
1968—United States	42.8*
1972—W. Germany	42.8*

4 × 400-METER RELAY

1972—E. Germany	3:23.0*

80-METER HURDLES

	Sec.
1932—Mildred Didrikson, U.S.A.	11.7
1936—Trebisonda Valla, Italy	11.7
1948—Francina Blankers-Koen, Netherlands	11.2
1952—Shirley Strickland de la Hunty, Australia	10.9
1956—Shirley de la Hunty, Australia	10.7
1960—Irina Press, U.S.S.R.	10.8
1964—Karen Balzer, Germany	10.5
1968—M. Caird, Australia	10.3*
1972—Ann Ehrhardt, E. Germany	12.6†

†Event run at 100 meters.

200 METERS

	Sec.
1948—Francina Blankers-Koen, Netherlands	24.4
1952—Marjorie Jackson, Australia	23.7
1956—Betty Cuthbert, Australia	23.4
1960—Wilma Rudolph, U.S.A.	24.0
1964—Edith McGuire, U.S.A.	23.0
1968—I. Kirszenstein, Poland	22.5
1972—Renate Stecher, E. Germany	22.4*

400 METERS

	Sec.
1964—Betty Cuthbert, Australia	52.0
1968—Colette Besson, France	52.0
1972—Monika Zehrt, E. Germany	51.1*

*Indicates Olympic record

LONG JUMP

1948—Olga Gyarmati, Hungary	18'	8¼"

1952—Yvette Williams, N. Zealand 20' 5¾"
1956—Elzbieta Krzesinska, Poland 20' 9¾"
1960—Vera Krepkina, U.S.S.R. 20' 10¾"
1964—Mary Rand, Great Britain 22' 2"
1968—V. Viscopoleanu, Rumania 22' 4½"*
1972—Heide Rosendahl,
    W. Germany 22' 3"

HIGH JUMP

1928—Ethel Catherwood, Canada 5' 3"
1932—Jean Shiley, U.S.A. 5' 4¹⁵⁄₁₆"
1936—Ibolya Csak, Hungary 5' 3"
1948—Alice Coachman, U.S.A. 5' 6¼"
1952—Esther Brand, So. Africa 5' 5¾"
1956—Mildred McDaniel, U.S.A. 5' 9¼"
1960—Ioland Balas, Rumania 6' 0¾"
1964—I. Balas, Rumania 6' 2¾"
1968—M. Rezkova, Czech. 5' 11¾"
1972—Ulrike Meyfarth,
    W. Germany 6' 3¼"*

SHOT PUT

1948—Micheline Ostermeyer,
    France 45' 1½"
1952—Galina Zybina, U.S.S.R. 50' 1½"
1956—Tamara Tishkyevich,
    U.S.S.R. 54' 5"
1960—Tamara Press, U.S.S.R. 56' 9¾"
1964—Tamara Press, U.S.S.R. 59' 6"
1968—Margitta Gummell,
    E. Germany 64' 4"
1972—Nadezhda Chizhova,
    U.S.S.R. 69' 0"*

DISCUS THROW

1928—Helena Konopacka, Poland 129' 11⅞"
1932—Lillian Copeland, U.S.A. 133' 1⅝"
1936—Gisela Mauermayer,
    Germany 156' 3³⁄₁₆"
1948—Micheline Ostermeyer,
    France 137' 6½"
1952—Nina Romaschkova,
    U.S.S.R. 168' 8½"
1956—Olga Fikotova, Czech. 176' 1½"
1960—Nina Romaschkova,
    Ponomareva, U.S.S.R. 180' 8¼"
1964—Tamara Press, U.S.S.R. 187' 10¾"

*Indicates Olympic record

1968—L. Manoliv, Rumania 191' 2½"
1972—Fania Melnik, U.S.S.R. 218' 7"*

JAVELIN THROW

1932—Mildred Didrikson, U.S.A. 143' 4"
1936—Tilly Fleischer, Germany 148' 2¾"
1948—Herma Bauma, Austria 149' 6"
1952—Dana Zatopekova, Czech. 165' 7"
1956—Inessa Janzeme, U.S.S.R. 176' 8"
1960—Elvira Ozolina, U.S.S.R. 183' 8"
1964—Mihaela Penes, Rumania 198' 7½"
1968—Angela Nemeth, Hungary 198' 7½"
1972—Ruth Fuchs, E. Germany 209' 7"*

PENTATHLON†

1964—Irina Press, U.S.S.R.
1968—I. Becker, W. Germany
1972—Mary Peters, Gt. Britain
    †Scoring systems subject to change.

BASKETBALL

1936—United States
1938—United States
1952—United States
1956—United States
1960—United States
1964—United States
1968—United States
1972—U.S.S.R.

BOXING
Light Flyweight

1968—Fran Rodriguez, Venezuela
1972—Gyoergy Gedeo, Hungary

Flyweight

1904—George V. Finnegan, U.S.A.
1920—Frank Genaro, U.S.A.
1924—Fidel La Barba, U.S.A.
1928—Anton Kocsis, Hungary
1932—Stephen Enekes, Hungary
1936—Will Kaiser, Germany
1948—Pascuel Perez, Argentina

1952—Nate Brooks, U.S.A.
1956—Terence Spinks, Gt. Britain
1960—G. Torck, Hungary
1964—Fernando Atzori, Italy
1968—Ricardo Delgado, Mexico
1972—G. Kostadinov, Bulgaria

Bantamweight

1904—O. L. Kirk, U.S.A.
1908—H. Thomas, Gt. Britain
1920—Walker, So. Africa
1924—W. H. Smith, So. Africa
1928—Vittorio Tamagnini, Italy
1932—Horace Gwynne, Canada
1936—Ulderico Sergo, Italy
1948—T. Csik, Hungary
1952—Pentti Hamalainen, Finland
1956—Wolfgang Behrendt, Germany
1960—O. Grigoryev, U.S.S.R.
1964—Takao Sakurai, Japan
1968—Valery Sokolov, U.S.S.R.
1972—Orlando Martinez, Cuba

Featherweight

1904—O. L. Kirk, U.S.A.
1908—R. K. Gunn, Gt. Britain
1920—Fritsch, France
1924—Jack Fields, U.S.A.
1928—L. Van Klaveren, Holland
1932—Carmelo Robledo, Argentina
1936—Oscar Casanoras, Argentina
1948—Ernesto Formenti, Italy
1952—Jan Zachara, Czechoslovakia
1956—Vladimir Sefronov, U.S.S.R.
1960—F. Musso, Italy
1964—Stanislav Stepashkin, U.S.S.R.
1968—Antonio Roldan, Mexico
1972—Boris Kousnetsov, U.S.S.R.

Lightweight

1904—H. J. Spenger, U.S.A.
1908—F. Grace, Gt. Britain
1920—Samuel Mosberg, U.S.A.
1924—Harold Nielsen, Denmark
1928—Carlo Orlandi, Italy
1932—Lawrence Stevens, So. Africa
1936—Imre Harangi, Hungary
1948—Jerry Dreyer, So. Africa
1952—Aureliano Bolognesi, Italy
1956—Richard McTaggart, Gt. Britain
1960—K. Pazdzier, Poland
1964—Jozef Grudzein, Poland
1968—Ronnie Harris, U.S.A.
1972—Jan Szczepanski, Poland

Light Welterweight

1952—Charles Adkins, U.S.A.
1956—Vladimir Engoibarian, U.S.S.R.
1960—B. Nemecek, Czechoslovakia
1964—Jerzy Kulei, Poland
1968—Jerzy Kulei, Poland
1972—Ray Seales, U.S.A.

Welterweight

1904—Al Young, U.S.A.
1920—Schneider, Canada
1924—J. S. DeLarge, Belgium
1928—Edward Morgan, New Zealand
1932—Edward Flynn, U.S.A.
1936—Sten Suvio, Finland
1948—Julius Torma, Czechoslovakia
1952—Zygmunt Chychia, Poland
1956—Necolae Linca, Rumania
1960—Giovanni Benvenuti, Italy
1964—Giovanni Benvenuti, Italy
1968—Manfred Wolke, E. Germany
1972—Emil Correa, Cuba

Light Middleweight

1952—Laszlo Papp, Hungary
1956—Laszlo Papp, Hungary
1960—Wilbur McClure, U.S.A.
1964—Marian Kasprzyk, Poland
1968—Boris Lagutin, U.S.S.R.
1972—Dieter Kottysch, W. Germany

Middleweight

1904—Charles Mayer, U.S.A.
1908—J. W. N. T. Douglas, Gt. Britain
1920—H. W. Mallin, Gt. Britain

1924—H. W. Mallin, Gt. Britain
1928—Piero Toscani, Italy
1932—Carmen Barth, U.S.A.
1936—Jean Despeaux, France
1948—Laszlo Papp, Hungary
1952—Floyd Patterson, U.S.A.
1956—Guennaddi Chatkov, U.S.S.R.
1960—Eddie Crook, U.S.A.
1964—Valery Popenchenko, U.S.S.R.
1968—Chris Finnegan, Gt. Britain
1972—V. Lemechev, U.S.S.R.

Light Heavyweight

1920—Edward Eagan, U.S.A.
1924—H. J. Mitchell, Gt. Britain
1928—Victor Avendano, Argentina
1932—David E. Carstens, So. Africa
1936—Roger Michelot, France
1948—George Hunter, So. Africa
1952—Norvel Lee, U.S.A.
1956—James Boyd, U.S.A.
1960—Cassius Clay, U.S.A.
1964—Cosimo Pinto, Italy
1968—Dan Rozniak, U.S.S.R.
1972—Mate Parlov, Yugoslavia

Heavyweight

1904—Sam Berger, U.S.A.
1908—A. L. Oldham, Gt. Britain
1920—Rawson, Gt. Britain
1924—Otto Von Porath, Norway
1928—J. Rodriguez Jurado, Argentina
1932—Santiago A. Lovell, Argentina
1936—Herbert Runge, Germany
1948—Rafael Iglesias, Argentina
1952—Edward Sanders, U.S.A.
1956—Pete Rademacher, U.S.A.
1960—F. De Piccoli, Italy
1964—Joe Frazier, U.S.A.
1968—George Foreman, U.S.A.
1972—Teofilo Stevenson, Cuba

CANOEING—MEN
Kayak Singles 1,000 Meters

1936—Gregor Hradetzky, Austria

1948—Gert Fredriksson, Sweden
1952—Gert Fredriksson, Sweden
1956—Gert Fredriksson, Sweden
1960—F. Hansen, Denmark
1964—Rolf Peterson, Sweden
1968—Mihaly Hesz, Hungary
1972—A. Shaparenko, U.S.S.R.

Canadian Singles 1,000 Meters

1936—Francis Amyot, Canada
1948—Josef Holecek, Czechoslovakia
1952—Josef Holecek, Czechoslovakia
1956—Leon Rottman, Rumania
1960—J. Parti, Hungary
1964—Jurgen Eschert, Germany
1968—Tibor Tatai, Hungary
1972—I. Patzaichin, Rumania

Kayak Pairs, 1,000 Meters

1936—Austria (Adolf Kainz, Alfons Dorfner)
1948—Sweden (H. Berglund, L. Klingstroem)
1952—Finland (K. Wires, Y. Hietanen)
1956—Germany (M. Scheur, M. Miltenberger)
1960—Sweden (G. Fredriksson, S, Sjodelius)
1964—Sweden (S. Sjodelius, G. Utterber)
1968—U.S.S.R. (Shaparenko, Morazov)
1972—U.S.S.R. (Gorbachev, Kratassyuk)

Canadian Pairs 1,000 Meters

1936—Czechoslovakia (V. Syrovatka, F. Jan Brzak)
1948—Czechoslovakia (J. Brzak, B. Kudrna)
1952—Denmark (B. Rasch, F. Haunstoft)
1956—Rumania (A. Dumitru, S. Ismailciuc)
1960—U.S.S.R. (L. Geyshter, S. Makarenko)
1964—U.S.S.R. (A. Khimich, S. Oschepkov)
1968—Rumania (Patzaichin, Covallov)
1972—U.S.S.R. (Chessyunas, Lobanov)

Kayak Fours

1968—Norway (Amundsen, Berger, Soby, Johansen)
1972—U.S.S.R. (Filatov, Stezenko, Morozov, Didenko)

CANOEING—WOMEN
Kayak Singles 500 Meters

1948—K. Hoff, Denmark
1952—Sylvia Saimo, Finland
1956—Elisavota Dementieva, U.S.S.R.
1960—A. Seredina, U.S.S.R.
1964—L. Khvedosink, U.S.S.R.
1968—Ludmilla Pinaeva, U.S.S.R.
1972—Y. Ryabchinskaya, U.S.S.R.

Kayak Pairs 500 Meters

1960—Russia (M. Shabina, A. Seredina)
1964—W. Germany (R. Esser, A. Zimmermann)
1968—W. Germany (R. Esser, A. Zimmermann)
1972—U.S.S.R. (Pinaeva, Kuryshko)

CYCLING
Road Race, Individual

1896—Konstantinidis, Greece
1906—Vast and Bardonneau (tie), France
1912—R. Lewis, South Africa
1920—H. Stenquist, Sweden
1924—A. Blanchonnet, France
1928—H. Hansen, Denmark
1932—Attilio Pavesl, Italy
1936—R. Charpentier, France
1948—J. Bayaert, France
1952—Andrae Noyelle, Belgium
1956—Ercole Baldini, Italy
1960—V. Kapitonov, U.S.S.R.
1964—M. Zanin, Italy
1968—P. Vianelli, Italy
1972—H. Kuiper, Netherlands

Road Race, Team

1912—Sweden
1920—France
1924—France
1928—Denmark
1932—Italy
1936—France
1948—Belgium
1952—Belgium
1956—France
1960—Italy
1964—Holland
1968—Holland
1972—U.S.S.R.

1,000-Meter Scratch

1896—Emile Masson, France†
1900—Taillendier, France
1906—Francesco Verri, Italy
1908—Void, time limit exceeded
1920—Maurice Peeters, Holland
1924—Lucien Michard, France
1928—R. Beaufrand, France
1932—Jacobus van Edmond, Holland
1936—Toni Merkens, Germany
1948—Mario Ghella, Italy‡
1952—Enzo Sacchi, Italy
1956—Michel Rousseau, France
1960—S. Gaiardoni, Italy
1964—G. Pattenella, Italy
1968—D. Morelon, France
1972—D. Morelon, France
†2,000 meters.
‡920 meters.

2,000-Meter Tandem

1906—Great Britain (Matthews, Rushen)
1908—France (Schilles, Auffray)
1920—Great Britain (Ryan, Lance)
1924—France (Choury, Cugnot)
1928—Holland (Leene, van Dijk)
1932—France (Perrin, Chaillot)
1936—Germany (Ihbe, Lorenz)
1948—Italy (Teruzzi, Perona)
1952—Australia (Cox, Mockridge)
1956—Australia (Brown, Marchant)
1960—Italy (Beghetto, Bianchetto)
1964—Italy (A. Damiano, S. Bianchetto)
1968—France (D. Morelon, P. Trentin)
1972—U.S.S.R. (Semenets, Tselovalnikov)

4,000-Meter Team Pursuit

1908—Great Britain (1,980 yards)
1920—Italy
1924—Italy
1928—Italy
1932—Italy
1936—France

Gold Medal Winners Summer Olympics 1892–1972 / *157*

1948—France
1952—Italy
1956—Italy
1960—Italy
1964—Germany
1968—Denmark
1972—W. Germany

1,000-Meter Time Trial

1928—W. Falck-Hansen, Denmark
1932—E. L. Gray, Australia
1936—Arie Gerrit van Vliet, Holland
1948—J. Dupont, France
1952—Russell Mockridge, Australia
1956—Leonardo Faggin, Italy
1960—S. Gaiardoni, Italy
1964—Patrick Sercu, Belgium
1968—P. Trentin, France
1972—N. Fredborg, Denmark

4,000-Meter Pursuit, Individual

1964—J. Daler, Czechoslovakia
1968—D. Rebillard, France
1972—Knut Knudsen, Norway

EQUESTRIAN
3-Day Event, Individual

1912—Lt. A. Nordlander, Sweden
1920—Lt. H. Morner, Sweden
1924—A. D. C. Van Der Voort Van Zijp, Holland
1928—Lt. C. F. Pahud de Mortanges, Holland
1932—de Mortanges, Holland
1936—Ludwig Stubbendorff, Germany
1948—Capt. B. Chevallier, France
1952—Hans von Blixen-Finecke, Sweden
1956—Lt. Petrus Kastenman, Sweden
1960—L. R. Morgan, Australia
1964—M. Checcoli, Italy
1968—J. J. Guyon, France
1972—Richard Meade, Gt. Britain

3-Day Event, Team

1912—Sweden
1920—Sweden

1924—Holland
1928—Holland
1932—United States
1936—Germany
1948—United States
1952—Sweden
1956—Great Britain
1960—Australia
1964—Italy
1968—Great Britain
1972—Great Britain

Dressage, Individual

1912—Capt. C. Bonde, Sweden
1920—Capt. Lundblad, Sweden
1924—E. V. Linder, Sweden
1928—C. F. von Langen, Germany
1932—F. Lesage, France
1936—H. Pollay, Germany
1948—Capt. H. Moser, Switzerland
1952—Major Henri St. Cyr, Sweden
1956—Major Henri St. Cyr, Sweden
1960—S. Filatov, U.S.S.R.
1964—H. Chammartin, Switzerland
1968—Ivan Kozomov, U.S.S.R.
1972—L. Lisenhoff, W. Germany

Dressage, Team

1928—Germany
1932—France
1936—Germany
1948—France
1952—Sweden
1956—Sweden
1960—None
1964—West Germany
1968—West Germany
1972—U.S.S.R.

Prix Des Nations, Individual

1912—Capt. J. Cariou, France
1920—Lt. Lequio, Italy
1924—Lt. Gemuseus, Switzerland
1928—F. Ventura, Czechoslovakia
1932—Takeichi Nishi, Japan
1936—Kurt Hasse, Germany

1948—Col. H. Mariles, Mexico
1952—Pierre d'Oriola, France
1956—Hans Winkler, Germany
1960—R. D'Inzeo, Italy
1964—Pierre d'Oriola, France
1968—W. Steinkraus, U.S.A.
1972—G. Mancinelli, Italy

Prix Des Nations, Team

1912—Sweden
1920—Sweden
1924—Sweden
1928—Spain
1932—All teams participating disqualified
1936—Germany
1948—Mexico
1952—Great Britain
1956—Germany
1960—Germany
1964—W. Germany
1968—Canada
1972—W. Germany

FENCING—MEN
Foil, Individual

1896—E. Gravelotte, France
1900—C. Coste, France
1904—Ramon Fonst, Cuba
1908—Not on program
1912—Nedo Nadi, Italy
1920—Nedo Nadi, Italy
1924—Roger Ducret, France
1928—Ludien Gaudin, France
1932—Gustavo Marzi, Italy
1936—Giulio Gaudini, Italy
1948—Jean Buhan, France
1952—Christian d'Oriola, France
1956—Christian d'Oriola, France
1960—Viktor Zhanovich, U.S.S.R.
1964—Egon Franke, Poland
1968—Ion Drima, Rumania
1972—Witold Woyda, Poland

Foil, Team

1904—Cuba
1908—Not on program
1912—Not on program
1920—Italy
1924—France
1928—Italy
1932—France
1936—Italy
1948—France
1952—France
1956—Italy
1960—U.S.S.R.
1964—U.S.S.R.
1968—France
1972—Poland

Epee, Individual

1900—Ramon Fonst, Cuba
1904—Ramon Fonst, Cuba
1908—Gaston Alibert, France
1912—Paul Anspach, Belgium
1920—Armand Massard, France
1924—Charles Delporte, Belgium
1928—Lucien Gaudin, France
1932—Giancarlo Cornaggia-Medici, Italy
1936—Franco Riccardi, Italy
1948—Luigi Cantone, Italy
1952—Edoardo Mangiarotti, Italy
1956—Carlo Pavesi, Italy
1960—Giuseppe Delfino, Italy
1964—Grigroy Kriss, U.S.S.R.
1968—Gyozo Kulcsar, Hungary
1972—Csaba Fenyvesi, Hungary

Epee, Team

1908—France
1912—Belgium
1920—Italy
1924—France
1928—Italy
1932—France
1936—Italy

1948—France
1952—Italy
1956—Italy
1960—Italy
1964—Hungary
1972—Hungary

Sabre, Individual

1896—Jean Georgiadis, Greece
1900—Count G. de la Falaise, France
1904—Manuel Diaz, Cuba
1908—Dr. Jeno Fuchs, Hungary
1912—Dr. Jeno Fuchs, Hungary
1920—Nedo Nadi, Italy
1924—Sandor Posta, Hungary
1928—Odon Tersztyanszky, Hungary
1932—Gyorgy Piller, Hungary
1936—Endre Kabos, Hungary
1948—Aladar Gerevich, Hungary
1952—Pal Kovacs, Hungary
1956—Rudolf Karpati, Hungary
1960—Rudolf Karpati, Hungary
1924—Sandor Posta, Hungary
1968—Jerzy Pawlowski, Poland
1972—Victor Sidiak, U.S.S.R.

Sabre, Team

1908—Hungary
1912—Hungary
1920—Italy
1924—Italy
1928—Hungary
1932—Hungary
1936—Hungary
1948—Hungary
1952—Hungary
1956—Hungary
1960—Hungary
1964—U.S.S.R.
1968—U.S.S.R.
1972—Italy

FENCING—WOMEN
Foil, Individual

1924—Mrs. Ellen Osiier, Denmark
1928—Helene Mayer, Germany
1932—Ellen Preis, Austria
1936—Ilona Schacherer-Elek, Hungary
1948—Ilona Schacherer-Elek, Hungary
1952—Irene Camber, Italy
1956—Gillian Sheen, Great Britain
1960—Adelheid Schmid, Germany
1964—Ildiko Ujlaki Rejto, Hungary
1968—Elene Novikova, U.S.S.R.
1972—Antonella Lonzi, Italy

Foil, Team

1960—U.S.S.R.
1964—Hungary
1968—U.S.S.R.
1972—U.S.S.R.

FIELD HOCKEY

1908—Great Britain
1912—Great Britain
1920—Great Britain
1928—India
1932—India
1936—India
1948—India
1952—India
1956—India
1960—Pakistan
1964—India
1968—Pakistan
1972—W. Germany

GYMNASTICS—MEN
All-Around Individual

1900—S. Sandras, France
1904—Anton Heida, United States
1908—Alberto Braglia, Italy
1912—Alberto Braglia, Italy
1920—Giorgio Zampori, Italy

1924—Leon Stukelj, Yugoslavia
1928—George Miez, Switzerland
1932—Romeo Neri, Italy
1936—Alfred Schwarzmann, Germany
1948—Veikko Huhtanen, Finland
1952—Viktor Chukarin, U.S.S.R.
1956—Viktor Chukarin, U.S.S.R.
1960—Boris Shakhlin, U.S.S.R.
1964—Yukio Endo, Japan
1968—Sawao Kato, Japan
1972—Sawao Kato, Japan

Long Horse Vault

1896—Karl Schumann, Germany
1904—Anton Heida and George Eyser, United States
1924—Frank Kriz, United States
1928—Eagen Mack, Switzerland
1932—Savino Guglielmetti, Italy
1936—Karl Schwarzmann, Germany
1948—Paavo Aaltonen, Finland
1952—Viktor Chukarin, U.S.S.R.
1956—Helmuth Bantz, Germany, and Valentine Mouratov, U.S.S.R.
1960—Boris Shakhlin, U.S.S.R., and Takashi Ono, Japan
1964—Haruhiro Yamashita, Japan
1968—Mikhail Voronin, U.S.S.R.
1972—Klaus Koeste, E. Germany

Pommelled (Side) Horse

1896—Louis Zutter, Switzerland
1904—Anton Heida, United States
1924—Josef Wilhelm, Switzerland
1928—Hermann Hanggi, Switzerland
1932—Istvan Pelle, Hungary
1936—Konrad Frey, Germany
1948—Paavo Aaltonen, Finland, Veikko Huhtanen, Finland, and Heikki Savolainen, Finland
1952—Viktor Chukarin, U.S.S.R.
1956—Boris Shakhlin, U.S.S.R.
1960—Boris Shakhlin, U.S.S.R., and Eugen Ekman, Finland
1964—Miroslav Cerar, Yugoslavia
1968—Miroslav Cerar, Yugoslavia
1972—Viktor Klimenko, U.S.S.R.

Horizontal Bar

1896—Hermann Weingartner, Germany
1904—Anton Heida and E. A. Hennig, United States
1924—Leon Stukelj, Yugoslavia
1928—Georges Miez, Switzerland
1932—Dallas Bixler, United States
1936—Aleksanteri Saarvala, Finland
1948—Joseph Stalder, Switzerland
1952—Jack Gunthard, Switzerland
1956—Takashi Ono, Japan
1960—Takashi Ono, Japan
1964—Boris Shakhlin, U.S.S.R.
1968—Michael Voronin, U.S.S.R., and Akinori Nakayama, Japan
1972—Mitsuo Tsukahara, Japan

Parallel Bars

1896—Alfred Flatow, Germany
1904—George Eyser, United States
1924—August Guttinger, Switzerland
1928—Ladislav Vacha, Czechoslovakia
1932—Romeo Neri, Italy
1936—Konrad Frey, Germany
1948—Michael Reusch, Switzerland
1952—Hans Eugster, Switzerland
1956—Viktor Chukarin, U.S.S.R.
1960—Boris Shakhlin, U.S.S.R.
1964—Yukio Endo, Japan
1968—Akinori Nakayama, Japan
1972—Sawao Kato, Japan

Rings

1896—Jean Mitropulos, Greece
1904—Hermann T. Glass, United States
1924—Franco Martino, Italy
1928—Leon Stukelj, Yugoslavia
1932—George J. Gulack, United States
1936—Alois Hudec, Czechoslovakia
1948—Karl Frei, Switzerland
1952—Grant Shaguinyan, U.S.S.R.
1956—Albert Azarian, U.S.S.R.
1960—Albert Azarian, U.S.S.R.
1964—Takuji Hayata, Japan
1968—Akinori Nakayama, Japan
1972—A. Nakayama, Japan

Free Exercise

1936—Georges Miez, Switzerland
1948—Ferenc Pataki, Hungary
1952—Karl Thoresson, Sweden
1956—Valentine Mouratov, U.S.S.R.
1960—Nobuyuki Aihara, Japan
1964—Franco Menichelli, Italy
1968—Akinori Nakayama, Japan
1972—Nikolai Andrianov, U.S.S.R.

Team

1896—Germany
1904—United States
1908—Sweden
1912—Italy
1920—Italy
1924—Italy
1928—Switzerland
1932—Italy
1936—Germany
1948—Finland
1952—U.S.S.R.
1956—U.S.S.R.
1960—Japan
1964—Japan
1968—Japan
1972—Japan

GYMNASTICS—WOMEN
All-Around Individual

1952—Maria Gorokhovskaya, U.S.S.R.
1956—Larisa Latynina, U.S.S.R.
1960—Larisa Latynina, U.S.S.R.
1964—Vera Caslavska, Czech.
1968—Vera Caslavska, Czech.
1972—Ludmilla Turischeva, U.S.S.R.

Balance Beam

1952—Nina Bocharoka, U.S.S.R.
1956—Agnes Keleti, Hungary
1960—Eva Bosakova, Czech.
1964—Vera Caslavska, Czech.
1968—Natalia Kuchinskaya, U.S.S.R.
1972—Olga Korbut, U.S.S.R.

Uneven Parallel Bars

1952—Margit Korondi, Hungary
1956—Agnes Keleti, Hungary
1960—Polina Astakhova, U.S.S.R.
1964—Polina Astakhova, U.S.S.R.
1968—Vera Caslavska, Czech.
1972—Karin Janz, E. Germany

Long Horse Vault

1952—Yekaterina Kalinchuk, U.S.S.R.
1956—Larisa Latynina, U.S.S.R.
1960—Margarita Nikolaeva, U.S.S.R.
1964—Vera Caslavska, Czech.
1968—Vera Caslavska, Czech.
1972—Karin Janz, E. Germany

Free Exercise

1952—Agnes Keleti, Hungary
1956—Larisa Latynina, U.S.S.R.
1960—Larisa Latynina, U.S.S.R.
1964—Larisa Latynina, U.S.S.R.
1968—Vera Caslavska, Czech. and Larissa Petrik, U.S.S.R.
1972—Olga Korbut, U.S.S.R.

Team

1928—Netherlands
1936—Germany
1948—Czechoslovakia
1952—U.S.S.R.
1956—U.S.S.R.
1960—U.S.S.R.
1964—U.S.S.R.
1968—U.S.S.R.
1972—U.S.S.R.

MODERN PENTATHLON
Individual

1912—Gustaf Lilliehook, Sweden

1920—Gustaf Dyrssen, Sweden
1924—Bo Lindman, Sweden
1928—Sven Thofelt, Sweden
1932—Johan Oxenstierna, Sweden
1936—Gotthard Handrick, Germany
1948—Capt. William Grut, Sweden
1952—Lars Hall, Sweden
1956—Lars Hall, Sweden
1960—Ferenc Nemeth, Hungary
1964—Ferenc Torok, Hungary
1968—Bjoern Ferm, Sweden
1972—Andras Balezo, Hungary

Team†

1952—Hungary
1956—U.S.S.R.
1960—Hungary
1964—U.S.S.R.
1968—Hungary
1972—U.S.S.R.

†Official since 1952.

ROWING
Single Sculls

	Min.-Sec.
1900—H. Barrelet, France	7:35.6
1908—Harry Blackstaff, Gt. Britain	9:26.0
1912—William Kinnear, Gt. Britain	7:47.6
1920—John Kelly, U.S.A.	7:35.0
1924—Jack Beresford, Jr., Gt. Britain	7:49.2
1928—Henry Pearce, Australia	7:11.0
1932—Henry Pearce, Australia	7:44.4
1936—Gustav Schafer, Germany	8:21.5
1948—Mervyn Wood, Australia	7:24.4
1952—Yuri Chukalov, U.S.S.R.	8:12.8
1956—Vlacheslav Ivanov, U.S.S.R.	8:02.5
1960—Vlacheslav Ivanov, U.S.S.R.	7:13.96
1964—Vlacheslav Ivanov, U.S.S.R.	8:22.51
1968—Jan Henri Wienese, Netherlands	7:47.80
1972—Yuri Malishev, U.S.S.R.	7:10.12

Double Sculls

	Min.-Sec.
1920—United States (John Kelly, Sr., Paul Costello)	7:09.0
1924—United States (John Kelly, Sr., Paul Costello)	6:34.0
1928—United States (Paul Costello, Charles McIlvaine)	6:41.4
1932—United States (Kenneth Myers, Garrett Gilmore)	7:17.4
1936—Great Britain (Jack Beresford, Leslie Southwood)	7:20.8
1948—Great Britain (Richard Burnell, B. H. Bushnell)	6:51.3
1952—Argentina (Tranquilo Cappozzo, Eduardo Guerrero)	7:32.2
1956—U.S.S.R. (Alexander Berkoutov, Turi Tiukalov)	7:24.0
1960—Czechoslovakia (Vaclav Kozak, Pavel Schmidt)	6:47.50
1964—U.S.S.R. (Oleg Tiurin, Boris Dubrovsky)	7:10.66
1968—U.S.S.R. (Anatoly Sass, Alexander Timoshinin)	6:51.82
1972—U.S.S.R. (Alexander Timoshinin, Gennadi Korshikov)	7:01.77

Pairs without Coxswain

	Min.-Sec.
1908—Great Britain (J. Fenning, Gordon Thomson)	9:41.0
1920—Italy (Ercole Olgeni, Giovanni Scatturini)	7:56.0
1924—Netherlands (W. H. Rosingh, A. C. Beynen)	8:19.4
1928—Germany (Kurt Moeschter, Bruno Muller)	7:06.4
1932—Great Britain (Lewis Clive, H. R. Arthur Edwards)	8:00.0
1936—Germany (Willi Eichhorn, Hugo Strauss)	8:16.1
1948—Great Britain (J. H. Wilson, W. G. Laurie)	7:21.1
1952—United States (Charles Logg, Thomas Price)	8:20.7
1956—United States (James Fifer, Duvall Hecht)	7:55.4
1960—U.S.S.R. (Valentin Boreiko, Oleg Golovanou)	7:02.01
1964—Canada (George Hungerford, Roger Jackson)	7:32.94
1968—E. Germany (Jorge Lucke, Heinz Bothe)	7:26.56
1972—E. Germany (Siegfried Brietzke, Wolfgang Mager)	6:53.16

Gold Medal Winners Summer Olympics 1892–1972 / 163

Pairs with Coxswain

	Min.-Sec.
1900—Netherlands	7:34.2
1924—Switzerland	8:39.0
1928—Switzerland	7:42.6
1932—United States	8:25.8
1936—Germany	8:36.9
1948—Denmark	8:00.5
1952—France	8:28.6
1956—United States	8:26.1
1960—Germany	7:29.14
1964—United States	8:21.33
1968—Italy	8:04.81
1972—E. Germany	7:12.25

Fours without Coxswain

	Min.-Sec.
1908—Great Britain	8:34.0
1924—Great Britain	7:08.6
1928—Great Britain	6:36.0
1932—Great Britain	6:58.2
1936—Germany	7:01.8
1948—Italy	6:39.0
1952—Yugoslavia	7:16.0
1956—Canada	7:08.8
1960—United States	6:26.26
1964—Denmark	6:59.30
1968—E. Germany	6:39.18
1972—E. Germany	6:24.27

Fours with Coxswain

	Min.-Sec.
1900—Germany	5:59.0
1912—Germany	6:59.4
1920—Switzerland	6:54.0
1924—Switzerland	7:18.4
1928—Italy	6:47.8
1932—Germany	7:19.0
1936—Germany	7:16.2
1948—United States	6:50.3
1952—Czechoslovakia	7:33.4
1956—Italy	7:19.4
1960—Germany	6:39.12
1964—Germany	7:00.44
1968—New Zealand	6:45.62
1972—W. Germany	6:31.85

*Indicates Olympic record

Eight-Oar with Coxswain

	Min.-Sec.
1900—United States	6:09.8
1908—Great Britain	7:52.0
1912—Great Britain	6:15.0
1920—United States	6:02.6
1924—United States	6:33.4
1928—United States	6:03.2
1932—United States	6:37.6
1936—United States	6:25.4
1948—United States	5:56.7
1952—United States	6:25.9
1956—United States	6:35.2
1960—Germany	5:57.18
1964—United States	6:18.23
1968—W. Germany	6:07.00
1972—New Zealand	6:08.94

SHOOTING
Rapid-Fire Pistol (Silhouette)
25 METERS

1936—Cornelius van Oyen, Germany	36
1948—Karoly Takacs, Hungary	580
1952—Karoly Takacs, Hungary	579
1956—Stefan Petrescu, Rumania	587
1960—William McMillan, U.S.A.	587
1964—Pentti Linnosvuo, Finland	592
1968—Josef Zapedzki, Poland	593
1972—Josef Zapedzki, Poland	595*

Small-Bore Rifle—Prone
50 METERS

1912—Frederick Hird, United States	194 × 200
1928—Bertil Ronnmark, Sweden	294 × 300
1936—Willy Rogeberg, Norway	300 × 300
1948—Arthur Cook, U.S.A.	599 × 600
1952—Josef Sarbu, Rumania	400 × 400
1956—Gerald Ouellette, Canada	600 × 600
1960—Peter Kohnke, Germany	590 × 600
1964—Laszlo Hammerl, Hungary	597 × 600
1968—Jan Kurka, Czechoslovakia	598 × 600
1972—HoJun Li, N. Korea	599 × 600*

Small-Bore Rifle—3 Positions
50 METERS

1952—Erling Kongshaug, Norway	1,164
1956—Anatole Bogdanov, U.S.S.R.	1,172
1960—Viktor Shamburkin, U.S.S.R.	1,149
1964—Lones Wigger, Jr., U.S.A.	1,164

1968—Bernd Klinger, W. Germany 1,157
1972—John Writer, U.S.A. 1,166*

Free Rifle—3 Positions
300 METERS

1900—Emil Kellemberger, Switzerland	930
1908—Albert Helgernd, Norway	909
1912—P. R. Colas, France	987
1920—Morris Fisher, U.S.A.	996
1948—Emil Grunig, Switzerland	1,120
1952—Anatoli Bogdanov, U.S.S.R.	1,123
1956—Vassili Borissov, U.S.S.R.	1,138
1960—Hubert Hammerer, Australia	1,129
1964—Gary Anderson, U.S.A.	1,153
1968—Gary Anderson, U.S.A.	1,157*
1972—Lorne Wigger, U.S.A.	1,155

Skeet Shooting

1968—Evgeny Petrov, U.S.S.R. 198*
1972—K. Wirnhier, W. Germany 195

Trapshooting (Clay Pigeons)
INDIVIDUAL

	Points
1908—W. H. Ewing, Canada	72 × 80
1912—James Graham, U.S.A.	96 × 100
1920—Mark Arie, U.S.A.	95 × 100
1924—Gyula Halasy, Hungary	98 × 100
1952—George Genereux, Canada	192 × 200
1956—Galliano Rossini, Italy	195 × 200
1960—Ion Dumitrescu, Rumania	192 × 200
1964—Ennio Mattarelli, Italy	198 × 200
1968—John Braithwaite, Gt. Britain	198 × 200
1972—A. Scalzone, Italy	199 × 200*

Free Pistol
50 METERS

1900—Roderer, Switzerland	503 × 600
1908—Paul van Asbrock, Belgium (50 yds.)	490
1912—Alfred Lane, U.S.A.	499
1920—Karl Frederick, U.S.A.	496
1936—Thorsten Ullman, Sweden	539
1948—E. Vasquez Cam, Peru	545
1952—Huelet Benner, U.S.A.	553
1956—Pentti Linnosvuoo, Finland	556
1960—Alexei Gustchin, U.S.S.R.	560
1964—Vaino Markkanen, Finland	560

*Indicates Olympic record

1968—Grigory Kosykh, U.S.S.R. 562
1972—Ragnar Skanaker, Sweden 567*

SOCCER (FOOTBALL)

1900—Great Britain
1904—Canada
1908—Great Britain
1912—Great Britain
1920—Belgium
1924—Uruguay
1928—Uruguay
1932—Not on program
1936—Italy
1948—Sweden
1952—Hungary
1956—U.S.S.R.
1960—Yugoslavia
1964—Hungary
1968—Hungary
1972—Poland

SWIMMING AND DIVING—MEN
100 Meters Freestyle

	Min.-Sec.
1896—Alfred Hajos, Hungary	1:22.2
1904—(yrds.) Zoltan de Halmay, Hungary	1:02.8
1908—Charles Daniels, U.S.A.	1:05.6
1912—Duke Kahanamoku, U.S.A.	1:03.4
1920—Duke Kahanamoku, U.S.A.	1:00.4
1924—John Weissmuller, U.S.A.	:59.0
1928—John Weissmuller, U.S.A.	:58.6
1932—Yasuji Miyazaki, Japan	:58.2
1936—Ferenc Csik, Hungary	:57.6
1948—Walter Ris, U.S.A.	:57.3
1952—Clark Scholes, U.S.A.	:57.4
1956—Jon Henricks, Australia	:55.4
1960—John Devitt, Australia	:55.2
1964—Donald Schollander, U.S.A.	:53.4
1968—Mike Welden, Australia	:52.2
1972—Mark Spitz, U.S.A.	:51.2*

200 Meters Freestyle

	Min.-Sec.
1900—Frederick Lane, Australia	1:55.2
1968—Mike Welden, Australia	1:55.2
1972—Mark Spitz, U.S.A.	1:52.8*

Gold Medal Winners Summer Olympics 1892–1972 / 165

400 Meters Freestyle

	Min.-Sec.
1896—(500 m.) Paul Neumann, Austria	8:12.6
1904—(440 y.) Charles Daniels, U.S.A.	6:16.2
1908—Henry Taylor, Great Britain	5:36.8
1912—George Hodgson, Canada	5:24.4
1920—Norman Ross, U.S.A.	5:26.8
1924—John Weissmuller, U.S.A.	5:04.2
1928—Albert Zorilla, Argentina	5:01.6
1932—Clarence Crabbe, U.S.A.	4:48.4
1936—Jack Medica, U.S.A.	4:44.5
1948—William Smith, U.S.A.	4:41.0
1952—Jean Boiteux, France	4:30.7
1956—Murray Rose, Australia	4:27.3
1960—Murray Rose, Australia	4:18.3
1964—Donald Schollander, U.S.A.	4:12.2
1968—Michael Burton, U.S.A.	4:09.0
1972—Bradford Cooper, Australia	4:00.3*

1,500 Meters Freestyle

	Min.-Sec.
1896—(1,200 m.) Alfred Hajos, Hungary	18:22.2
1900—(1,000 m.) John Jarvis, Great Britain	13:40.2
1904—(1,609 m.) Emil Rausch, Germany	27:18.2
1908—Henry Taylor, Great Britain	22:48.4
1912—George Hodgson, Canada	22.00.0
1920—Norman Ross, U.S.A.	22:23.2
1924—Andrew Charlton, Australia	20:06.6
1928—Arne Borg, Sweden	19:51.8
1932—Kusuo Kitamura, Japan	19:12.4
1936—Noboru Terada, Japan	19:13.7
1948—James McLane, U.S.A.	19:18.5
1952—Ford Konno, U.S.A.	18:30.0
1956—Murray Rose, Australia	17:58.9
1960—Jon Konrads, Australia	17:19.6
1964—Robert Windle, Australia	17:01.7
1968—Michael Burton, U.S.A.	16:38.9
1972—Michael Burton, U.S.A.	15:52.6*

100 Meters Backstroke

	Min.-Sec.
1904—(yds.) Walter Brack, Germany	1:16.8
1908—Arno Bieberstein, Germany	1:24.6
1912—Harry Hebner, U.S.A.	1:21.2
1920—Warren Kealoha, U.S.A.	1:15.2
1924—Warren Kealoha, U.S.A.	1:13.2
1928—George Kojac, U.S.A.	1:08.2
1932—Masaji Kiyokawa, Japan	1:08.6
1936—Adolph Kiefer, U.S.A.	1:05.9
1948—Allen Stack, U.S.A.	1:06.4
1952—Yoshinobu Oyakawa, U.S.A.	1:05.4
1956—David Thiele, Australia	1:02.2
1960—David Thiele, Australia	1:01.9
1968—Roland Matthes, E. Germany	:58.7
1972—Roland Matthes, E. Germany	:56.6*

200 Meters Backstroke

	Min.-Sec.
1900—Ernst Hoppenberg, Germany	2:47.0
1964—Jed Graef, U.S.A.	2:10.3
1968—Roland Matthes, E. Germany	2:09.6
1972—Roland Matthes, E. Germany	2:02.8*

100 Meters Butterfly

	Sec.
1968—Douglas Russell, U.S.A.	:55.9
1972—Mark Spitz, U.S.A.	:54.3*

200 Meters Butterfly

	Min.-Sec.
1956—William Yorzyk, U.S.A.	2:19.3
1960—Michael Troy, U.S.A.	2:12.8
1964—Kevin Berry, Australia	2:06.6
1968—Carl Robie, U.S.A.	2:08.7
1972—Mark Spitz, U.S.A.	2:00.7*

100 Meters Breaststroke

	Min.-Sec.
1968—Donald McKenzie, U.S.A.	1:07.7
1972—N. Taguchi, Japan	1:04.9*

200 Meters Breaststroke

	Min.-Sec.
1908—Frederick Holman, Gt. Britain	3:09.2
1912—Walter Bathe, Germany	3:01.8

*Indicates Olympic record

1920—Haken Malmroth, Sweden 3:04.4
1924—Robert Skelton, U.S.A. 2:56.6
1928—Yoshiyuki Tsuruta, Japan 2:48.8
1932—Yoshiyuki Tsuruta, Japan 2:45.4
1936—Tetsuo Hamuro, Japan 2:41.5
1948—Joseph Verdeur, U.S.A. 2:39.3
1952—John Davies, Australia 2:34.4
1956—Masura Furukawa, Japan 2:34.7
1960—William Mulliken, U.S.A. 2:37.4
1964—Ian O'Brien, Australia 2:27.8
1968—Felipe Munoz, Mexico 2:28.7
1972—John Hencken, U.S.A. 2:21.6*

200-Meter Individual Medley

	Min.-Sec.
1968—Charles Hickcox, U.S.A.	2:12.0
1972—Gunnar Larrsen, Sweden	2:07.2*

400-Meter Individual Medley

	Min.-Sec.
1964—Richard Roth, U.S.A.	4:45.4
1968—Charles Hickcox, U.S.A.	4:48.4
1972—Gunnar Larrsen, Sweden	4:32.0*

4 × 100-Freestyle Relay

	Min.-Sec.
1964—United States	3:33.2
1968—United States	3:31.7
1972—United States	3:26.4*

4 × 200-Meter Freestyle Relay

	Min.-Sec.
1908—Great Britain	10:55.6
1912—Australasia	10:11.2
1920—United States	10:04.4
1924—United States	9:53.4
1928—United States	9:36.2
1932—Japan	8:58.4
1936—Japan	8:51.5
1948—United States	8:46.0
1952—United States	8:31.1
1956—Australia	8:23.6
1960—United States	8:10.2
1964—United States	7:52.1
1968—United States	7:52.3
1972—United States	7:35.8*

*Indicates Olympic record

4 × 100-Meter Medley Relay

	Min.-Sec.
1960—United States	4:05.4
1964—United States	3:58.4
1968—United States	3:54.9
1972—United States	3:48.2*

Springboard Diving

1908—Albert Zurner, Germany
1912—Paul Guenther, Germany
1920—Louis Kuehn, U.S.A.
1924—Albert White, U.S.A.
1928—Pete Desjardin, U.S.A.
1932—Michael Galitzen, U.S.A.
1936—Richard Degener, U.S.A.
1948—Bruce Harlan, U.S.A.
1952—David Browning, U.S.A.
1956—Robert Clotworthy, U.S.A.
1960—Gary Tobian, U.S.A.
1964—Kenneth Sitzberger, U.S.A.
1968—Bernard Wrightson, U.S.A.
1972—Vladim Vasin, U.S.S.R.

Platform Diving

1904—Dr. G. E. Sheldon, U.S.A.
1908—Hjalmar Johansson, Sweden
1912—Erik Adlerz, Sweden
1920—Clarence Pinkston, U.S.A.
1924—Albert White, U.S.A.
1928—Pete Desjardins, U.S.A.
1932—Harold Smith, U.S.A.
1936—Marshall Wayne, U.S.A.
1948—Dr. Samuel Lee, U.S.A.
1952—Dr. Samuel Lee, U.S.A.
1956—Joaquin Capilla, Mexico
1960—Robert Webster, U.S.A.
1964—Robert Webster, U.S.A.
1968—Klaus Dibiasi, Italy
1972—Klaus Dibiasi, Italy

SWIMMING AND DIVING— WOMEN
100 Meters Freestyle

	Min.-Sec.
1912—Fanny Durack, Australasia	1:22.2
1920—Ethelda Bleibtrey, U.S.A.	1:13.6
1924—Ethel Lackie, U.S.A.	1:12.4

Gold Medal Winners Summer Olympics 1892–1972 / 167

1928—Albina Osipowich, U.S.A.	1:11.0
1932—Helene Madison, U.S.A.	1:06.8
1936—Hendrika Mastenbroek, Netherlands	1:05.9
1948—Greta Andersen, Denmark	1:06.3
1952—Katalin Szoke, Hungary	1:06.8
1956—Dawn Fraser, Australia	1:02.0
1960—Dawn Fraser, Australia	1:01.2
1964—Dawn Fraser, Australia	59.5
1968—Margo Jan Henne, U.S.A.	1:00.0
1972—Sandra Neilson, U.S.A.	58.6*

200 Meters Freestyle

	Min.-Sec.
1968—Deborah Meyer, U.S.A.	2:10.5
1972—Shane Gould, Australia	2:03.6*

400 Meters Freestyle

	Min.-Sec.
1920—(300 m.) Ethelda Bleibtrey, U.S.A.	4:34.0
1924—Martha Norelius, U.S.A.	6:02.2
1928—Martha Norelius, U.S.A.	5:42.8
1932—Helene Madison, U.S.A.	5:28.5
1936—Hendrika Mastenbroek, Netherlands	5:26.4
1948—Ann Curtis, U.S.A.	5:17.8
1952—Valeria Gyenge, Hungary	5:12.1
1956—Lorraine Crapp, Australia	4:54.6
1960—Susan Chris Von Saltza, U.S.A.	4:50.6
1964—Virginia Duenkel, U.S.A.	4:43.3
1968—Deborah Meyer, U.S.A.	4:31.8
1972—Shane Gould, Australia	4:19.0*

800 Meters Freestyle

	Min.-Sec.
1968—Deborah Meyer, U.S.A.	9:24.0
1972—Keena Rothhammer, U.S.A.	8:53.7*

100 Meters Backstroke

	Min.-Sec.
1924—Sybil Bauer, U.S.A.	1:23.2
1928—Marie Braun, Netherlands	1:22.0
1932—Eleanor Holm, U.S.A.	1:19.4
1936—Dina Senff, Netherlands	1:18.9

*Indicates Olympic record

1948—Karen Harup, Denmark	1:14.4
1952—Joan Harrison, South Africa	1:14.3
1956—Judy Grinham, Great Britain	1:12.9
1960—Lynn Burke, U.S.A.	1:09.3
1964—Cathy Ferguson, U.S.A.	1:07.7
1968—Djurdjica Bjedov, Yugoslavia	1:15.8
1972—Melissa Belote, U.S.A.	1:05.8*

200 Meters Backstroke

	Min.-Sec.
1968—Lillian (Pokey) Watson, U.S.A.	2:24.8
1972—Melissa Belote, U.S.A.	2:19.2*

100 Meters Breaststroke

	Min.-Sec.
1968—Kaye Hall, U.S.A.	1:15.8
1972—Cathy Carr, U.S.A.	1:13.6*

200 Meters Breaststroke

	Min.-Sec.
1924—Lucy Morton, Great Britain	3:33.2
1928—Hilde Schrader, Germany	3:12.6
1932—Clare Dennis, Australia	3:06.3
1936—Hideko Maehata, Japan	3:03.6
1948—Petronella Van Vliet, Netherlands	2:57.2
1952—Eva Szekely, Hungary	2:51.7
1956—Ursula Happe, Germany	2:53.1
1960—Anita Lonsbrough, Great Britain	2:49.5
1964—Galina Prozumenschikova, U.S.S.R.	2:46.4
1968—Sharon Wichman, U.S.A.	2:44.4
1972—Beverly Whitfield, Australia	2:41.7*

100 Meters Butterfly

	Min.-Sec.
1956—Shelly Mann, U.S.A.	1:11.0
1960—Carolyn Schuler, U.S.A.	1:09.5
1964—Sharon Stouder, U.S.A.	1:04.7
1968—Lynn McClements, Australia	1:05.5
1972—Mayumi Aoki, Japan	1:03.3*

200 Meters Butterfly

	Min.-Sec.
1968—Ada Kok, Netherlands	2:24.7

1972—Karen Moe, U.S.A.   2:15.6*

200 Meters Individual Medley

	Min.-Sec.
1968—Claudia Kolb, U.S.A.	2:24.7
1972—Shane Gould, Australia	2:23.1*

400 Meters Individual Medley

	Min.-Sec.
1964—Donna de Varona, U.S.A.	5:18.7
1968—Claudia Kolb, U.S.A.	5:08.5
1972—Gail Neall, Australia	5:93.0*

4 × 100-Meter Freestyle Relay

	Min.-Sec.
1912—Great Britain	5:52.8
1920—United States	5:11.6
1924—United States	4:58.8
1928—United States	4:47.6
1932—United States	4:38.0
1936—Netherlands	4:36.0
1948—United States	4:29.2
1952—Hungary	4:24.4
1956—Australia	4:17.1
1960—United States	4:08.9
1964—United States	4:03.8
1968—United States	4:02.5
1972—United States	3:55.2*

4 × 100-Meter Medley Relay

1960—United States (Lynn Burke, Patty Kempner, Carolyn Schuler, S. Chris Von Saltza)	4:41.1
1964—United States (Cathy Ferguson, Cynthia Goyette, Sharon Stouder, Kathleen Ellis)	4:33.9
1968—United States (Kaye Hall, Catharine Ball, Eleanor Daniel, Sue Pedersen)	4:28.3
1972—United States	4:20.8*

Springboard Diving

1920—Aileen Riggin, U.S.A.
1924—Elizabeth Becker, U.S.A.

*Indicates Olympic record

1928—Helen Meany, U.S.A.
1932—Georgia Coleman, U.S.A.
1936—Majorie Gestring, U.S.A.
1948—Victoria Draves, U.S.A.
1952—Patricia McCormick, U.S.A.
1956—Patricia McCormick, U.S.A.
1960—Ingrid Kramer, Germany
1964—Ingrid Engel-Kramer, Germany
1968—Sue Gossick, U.S.A.
1972—Micki King, U.S.A.

Platform Diving

1912—Greta Johansson, Sweden
1920—Stefani Fryland-Clausen, Denmark
1924—Caroline Smith, U.S.A.
1928—Elizabeth Pinkston, U.S.A.
1932—Dorothy Poynton, U.S.A.
1936—Dorothy Poynton Hill, U.S.A.
1948—Victoria Draves, U.S.A.
1952—Patricia McCormick, U.S.A.
1956—Patricia McCormick, U.S.A.
1960—Ingrid Kramer, Germany
1964—Lesley Bush, United States
1968—Milena Duchkova, Czech.
1972—Olrika Knape, Sweden

VOLLEYBALL—MEN

1964—U.S.S.R.
1968—U.S.S.R.
1972—Japan

VOLLEYBALL—WOMEN

1964—Japan
1968—U.S.S.R.
1972—U.S.S.R.

WATER POLO

1900—Great Britain
1904—United States
1908—Great Britain
1912—Great Britain
1920—Great Britain
1924—France
1928—Germany
1932—Hungary

Gold Medal Winners Summer Olympics 1892–1972 / 169

1936—Hungary
1948—Italy
1952—Hungary
1956—Hungary
1960—Italy
1964—Hungary
1968—Yugoslavia
1972—U.S.S.R.

WEIGHTLIFTING
Bantamweight

	Pounds
1948—Jos. N. Depietro, U.S.A.	677.9
1952—Ivan Udodov, U.S.S.R.	694.5
1956—Charles Vinci, U.S.A.	754.5
1960—Charles Vinci, U.S.A.	760.0
1964—Alexei Vakhonin, U.S.S.R.	788.1
1968—Mohammed Nasiri Seresht, Iran	808.5
1972—I. Foeldi, Hungary	833.0*

Featherweight

1920—L. de Haes, Belgium	485.0
1924—Paolo Gabetti, Italy	See note
1928—Franz Andrysek, Austria	633.8
1932—Raymond Suvigny, France	633.8
1936—Anthony Terlazzo, U.S.A.	688.9
1948—Mahmoud Fayad, Egypt	733.0
1952—Rafael Chimishkyan, U.S.S.R.	743.5
1956—Isaac Berger, U.S.A.	776.5
1960—Evgeniy Minaev, U.S.S.R.	821.0
1964—Yoshinobu Miyake, Japan	876.3
1968—Yoshinobu Miyake, Japan	863.5
1972—N. Nourikian, Bulgaria	888.0*

Lightweight

1920—Alfred Neyland, Estonia	567.7
1924—Edmond Decottignies, France	See note
1928—Kurt Helbig, Germany, and Hans Hass, Austria	711.0
1932—Rene Duverger, France	716.5
1936—Mohammed Mesbah, Egypt, and Robert Fein, Austria	755.1
1948—Ibrahim Shams, Egypt	793.7
1952—Thomas Kono, U.S.A.	798.8
1956—Igors Rybak, U.S.S.R.	876.0
1960—Viktor Bushuev, U.S.S.R.	876.0

*Indicates Olympic record

1964—Waldemar Baszanowski, Poland — 953.5
1968—Waldemar Baszanowski, Poland — 962.5
1972—M. Kirzhinov, U.S.S.R. — 1,014.0*

Middleweight

1920—B. Gance, France	540.0
1924—Carlo Galimberti, Italy	See note
1928—Francois Roger, France	738.5
1932—Rudolf Ismayr, Germany	760.5
1936—Khadr El Thouni, Egypt	854.8
1948—Frank Spellman, U.S.A.	859.8
1952—Peter George, U.S.A.	881.5
1956—Fedor Bogdanovsky, U.S.S.R.	925.8
1960—Alexander Kurynov, U.S.S.R.	964.3
1964—Hans Zdrazila, Czechoslovakia	981.1
1968—Viktor Kurentsov, U.S.S.R.	1,045.0
1972—Y. Bikov, Bulgaria	1,069.0*

Light Heavyweight

1920—E. Cadine, France	639.3
1924—Charles Rigoulot, France	See note
1928—Saied Nosseir, Egypt	782.6
1932—Louis Hostin, France	804.7
1936—Louis Hostin, France	820.0
1948—Stanley Stanczyk, U.S.A.	920.4
1952—Trofim Lomakin, U.S.S.R.	920.3
1956—Thomas Kono, U.S.A.	986.3
1960—Iremeusz Palinski, Poland	975.3
1964—Rudolf Plyukfelder, U.S.S.R.	1,047.2
1968—Boris Selitsky, U.S.S.R.	1,067.0
1972—Lars Jenssen, Norway	1,118.0*

Middle Heavyweight

1952—Norbert Schemansky, U.S.A.	980.8
1956—Arkakiy Vorobiev, U.S.S.R.	1,019.3
1960—Arkakiy Vorobiev, U.S.S.R.	1,041.3
1964—Vladimir Golovanov, U.S.S.R.	1,074.7
1968—Kaarlo Kangasniemi, Finland	1,138.5
1972—A. Nikolov, Bulgaria	1,157.0*

Heavyweight

1920—Filippo Bottino, Italy	595.2

1924—Giuseppe Tonani, Italy — See note
1928—Josef Strassberger, Germany — 810.0
1932—Jaroslaw Skobia, Czechoslovakia — 837.7
1936—Josef Manger, Germany — 903.9
1948—John Davis, U.S.A. — 996.6
1952—John Davis, U.S.A. — 1,013.8
1956—Paul Anderson, U.S.A. — 1,102.0
1960—Yuriy Vlasov, U.S.S.R. — 1,184.3
1964—Leonid Zhabotinsky, U.S.S.R. — 1,272.1
1968—Leonid Zhabotinsky, U.S.S.R. — 1,259.5
1972—Y. Talts, U.S.S.R. — 1,278.0*

Super Heavyweight

1972—Vasila Alexeev, U.S.S.R. — 1,411.0*

Note: Special scoring system used in 1924 does not conform to present method.

WRESTLING, FREESTYLE
Paperweight

1972—Roman Dimitrev, U.S.S.R.

Flyweight

1904—Robert Curry, U.S.A.
1948—Lennart, Viitala, Finland
1952—Hasan Gemici, Turkey
1956—Mirian Tzalkalamanidze, U.S.S.R.
1960—Ahmet Bilek, Turkey
1964—Yoshikatsu Yoshida, Japan
1968—Shigeo Nakata, Japan
1972—Kiyomi Kato, Japan

Bantamweight

1904—George Mehnert, U.S.A.
1908—George Mehnert, U.S.A.
1924—Kustaa Pihlajamaki, Finland
1928—Kaarle Makinen, Finland
1932—Robert E. Pearce, U.S.A.
1936—Odon Zombori, Hungary
1948—Nasuh Akar, Turkey
1952—Shohachi, Ishii, Japan
1956—Mustafa Dagistanli, Turkey
1960—Terrence McCann, U.S.A.
1964—Yojiro Uetake, Japan

*Indicates Olympic record

1968—Yojiro Uetake, Japan
1972—H. Yanagida, Japan

Featherweight

1904—Isaac Niflot, U.S.A.
1908—George S. Dole, U.S.A.
1920—Charles E. Ackerly, U.S.A.
1924—Robin Reed, U.S.A.
1928—Allie Morrison, U.S.A.
1932—Hermanni Pihlajamaki, Finland
1936—Kustaa Pihlajamaki, Finland
1948—Gazanfer Bilge, Turkey
1952—Bayram Sit, Turkey
1956—Shozo Sashara, Japan
1960—Mustafa Dagistanli, Turkey
1964—Osamu Watanabe, Japan
1968—Masaaki Kaneko, Japan
1972—Z. Abdulbekov, U.S.S.R.

Lightweight

1904—Benjamin Bradshaw, U.S.A.
1908—G. de Relwyskow, Great Britain
1920—Kalle Antilla, Finland
1924—Russell Vis, U.S.A.
1928—Osvald Kapp, Estonia
1932—Charles Pacome, France
1936—Karoly Karpati, Hungary
1948—Celal Atik, Turkey
1952—Olle Anderberg, Sweden
1956—Emamli Habibi, Iran
1960—Shelby Wilson, U.S.A.
1964—Enio Dimov, Bulgaria
1968—Abdoliah Movahed, Iran
1972—Dan Gable, U.S.A.

Welterweight

1904—Otto F. Roehm, U.S.A.
1924—Hermann Gehri, Switzerland
1928—Arve J. Haavisto, Finland
1932—Jack F. Van Bebber, U.S.A.
1936—Frank Lewis, U.S.A.
1948—Yasar Dogu, Turkey
1952—William Smith, U.S.A.
1956—Mitsro Ikeda, Japan
1960—Douglas Blubaugh, U.S.A.
1964—Ismail Ogan, Turkey

1968—Mahmud Atalay, Turkey
1972—Wayne Wells, U.S.A.

1968—Aleksandr Medved, U.S.S.R.
1972—Ivan Yarygin, U.S.S.R.

Middleweight

1904—Charles Erickson, United States
1908—Stanley V. Bacon, Great Britain
1920—Eino Leino, Finland
1924—Fritz Haggmann, Switzerland
1928—Ernst Kyburz, Switzerland
1932—Ivar Johansson, Sweden
1936—Emile Poilve, France
1948—Glen Brand, U.S.A.
1952—David Cimakuridze, U.S.S.R.
1956—Nikola Nikolov, Bulgaria
1960—Hasan Gungor, Turkey
1964—Prodan Gardjev, Bulgaria
1968—Boris Gurevitch, U.S.S.R.
1972—L. Tediashvili, U.S.S.R.

Light-Heavyweight

1920—Anders Larsson, Sweden
1924—John Spellman, U.S.A.
1928—Thure Sjostedt, Sweden
1932—Peter J. Mehringer, U.S.A.
1936—Knut Fridell, Sweden
1948—Henry Wittenberg, U.S.A.
1952—Wiking Palm, Sweden
1956—Ghalam Takhiti, Iran
1960—Ismet Atli, Turkey
1964—Alexandr Medved, U.S.S.R.
1968—Ahmet Ayuk, Turkey
1972—Ben Peterson, U.S.A.

Heavyweight

1904—B. Hansen, U.S.A.
1908—G. C. O'Kelly, Great Britain
1920—Robert Roth, Switzerland
1924—Harry Steele, United States
1928—Johan C. Richthoff, Sweden
1932—Johan C. Richthoff, Sweden
1936—Kristjan Palusalu, Estonia
1948—Gyula Bobis, Hungary
1952—Arsen Mekokishvili, U.S.S.R.
1956—Haml Kaplan, Turkey
1960—Wilfried Dietrich, Germany
1964—Alexandr Ivanitsky, U.S.S.R.

Super Heavyweight

1972—Alexandr Medved, U.S.S.R.

WRESTLING, GRECO-ROMAN
Paperweight

1972—G. Berceanu, Rumania

Flyweight

1948—Pietro Lombardi, Italy
1952—Boris Gurevich, U.S.S.R.
1956—Nikolai Soloviev, U.S.S.R.
1960—Dumitru Pirvulescu, Rumania
1964—Tsutomu Hanahara, Japan
1968—Petar Kirov, Bulgaria
1972—Petar Kirov, Bulgaria

Bantamweight

1924—Eduard Putsep, Estonia
1928—Kurt Leucht, Germany
1932—Jakob Brendel, Germany
1936—Marton Lorinc, Hungary
1948—Kurt Pettersen, Sweden
1952—Imre Hodos, Hungary
1956—Konstantin Vyrorpaev, U.S.S.R.
1960—Oleg Karavaev, U.S.S.R.
1964—Masamitsu Ichiguchi, Japan
1968—Janos Varga, Hungary
1972—Rustem Kazakov, U.S.S.R.

Featherweight

1912—Kalle Koskelo, Finland
1920—Oskari Friman, Finland
1924—Kalle Anttila, Finland
1928—Voldemar Vali, Estonia
1932—Giovanni Gozzi, Italy
1936—Yasar Erkan, Turkey
1948—Mohammed Oktav, Turkey
1952—Yakov Punkin, U.S.S.R.
1956—Rauno Makinen, Finland
1960—Muzahir Sille, Turkey

1964—Imre Polyak, Hungary
1968—Roman Rurua, U.S.S.R.
1972—G. Markov, Bulgaria

Lightweight

1908—F. E. Porro, Italy
1912—Eemil Vare, Finland
1920—Eemil Vare, Finland
1924—Oscari, Friman, Finland
1928—Lajos Keresztes, Hungary
1932—Erik Malmberg, Sweden
1936—Lauri Koskela, Finland
1948—Karl Freij, Sweden
1952—Chasame Safin, U.S.S.R.
1956—Kyosti Lehtonen, Finland
1960—Avtandil Kordidze, U.S.S.R.
1964—Kazim Ayvaz, Turkey
1968—Muneji Mumemura, Japan
1972—S. Khisamutdinov, U.S.S.R.

Welterweight

1932—Ivar Johansson, Sweden
1936—Rudolf Svedberg, Sweden
1948—Gosta Andersson, Sweden
1952—Miklos Szilvasi, Hungary
1956—Mithat Bayrak, Turkey
1960—Mithat Bayrak, Turkey
1964—Anatoly Kolesov, U.S.S.R.
1968—Rudolph Vesper, East Germany
1972—V. Macha, Czechoslovakia

Middleweight

1908—Fritjof Martenson, Sweden
1912—Claes Johansson, Sweden
1920—Carl Westergren, Sweden
1924—Edvard Vesterlund, Finland
1928—Vaino A. Kokkinen, Finland
1932—Vaino A. Kokkinen, Finland
1936—Ivar Johansson, Sweden
1948—Axel Gronberg, Sweden
1952—Axel Gronberg, Sweden
1956—Vuiri Kartosa, U.S.S.R.
1960—Dimitro Dobrev, Bulgaria
1964—Branislav Simic, Yugoslavia

1968—Lothar Metz, East Germany
1972—Csaba Hegedus, Hungary

Light Heavyweight

1908—Verner Weckmann, Finland
1912—Anders Ahlgren, Sweden and
        Ivar Bohling, Finland (Tie)
1920—Claes Johansson, Sweden
1924—Carl Westergren, Sweden
1928—Ibrahim Moustafa, Egypt
1932—Rudolf Svensson, Sweden
1936—Axel Cadier, Sweden
1948—Karl Nilsson, Sweden
1952—Kaelpo Grondhal, Finland
1956—Valentine Nikolaev, U.S.S.R.
1960—Tevfik Kis, Turkey
1964—Boyan Alexandrov, Bulgaria
1968—Boyan Radev, Bulgaria
1972—Valeri Rezantsev, U.S.S.R.

Heavyweight

1896—Karl Schumann, Germany
1908—Richard Weisz, Hungary
1912—Yrjo Saarela, Finland
1920—Adolf Lindfors, Finland
1924—Henri Deglane, France
1928—J. Rudolph Svensson, Sweden
1936—Kristjan Palusalu, Estonia
1932—Carl Westergren, Sweden
1948—Ahmed Kirecci, Turkey
1952—Johannes Kotkas, U.S.S.R.
1956—Anatoli Parfenov, U.S.S.R.
1960—Ivan Bogdan, U.S.S.R.
1964—Istvan Kozma, Hungary
1968—Istvan Kozma, Hungary
1972—N. Martinescu, Rumania

Super Heavyweight

1972—Anatoly Roshin, U.S.S.R.

YACHTING
(Only helmsman's name listed.)
Soling Class

1972—Harry Melges, U.S.A.

Star Class

1932—Gilbert Gray, U.S.A.
1936—Dr. Peter Bischoff, Germany
1948—Hilary Smart, U.S.A.
1952—Agosto Straulino, Italy
1956—Herbert Williams, U.S.A.
1960—Timir Pinegin, U.S.S.R.
1964—Durward Knowles, Bahamas
1968—Lowell North, U.S.A.
1972—David Forbes, Australia

Finn Monotype Class

1952—Paul Elvstrom, Denmark
1956—P. Elvstrom, Denmark
1960—P. Elvstrom, Denmark
1964—Wilhelm Kuhweide, Germany
1968—Alentin Mankin, U.S.S.R.
1972—Serge Maury, France

Dragon Class

1948—Thor Thorvaldsen, Norway
1952—Thor Thorvaldsen, Norway
1956—Folke Bohlin, Sweden
1960—Constantino di Grecia, Greece
1964—Ole Bernsten, Denmark
1968—George Friedrichs, U.S.A.
1972—John Bruce, Australia

Flying Dutchman Class

1960—Peder Lunde, Norway
1964—Helmer Pedersen, New Zealand
1968—Rodney Pattisson, Great Britain
1972—R. Pattisson, Great Britain

Tempest Class

1972—Valentin Mankin, U.S.S.R.

GOLD MEDAL WINNERS
Winter Olympics 1924–1972

BIATHLON
Cross-Country Skiing and Marksmanship

1960—Klas Lestander, Sweden
1964—Vladimir Melanin, U.S.S.R.
1968—Magnar Solberg, Norway
1972—Magnar Solberg, Norway

4 × 10-Kilometer Relay

1968—U.S.S.R.
1972—U.S.S.R.

BOBSLED
Two-Man

1932—United States I*
1936—United States I
1948—Switzerland II
1952—Germany I
1956—Italy I
1960—Event not on program
1964—Great Britain
1968—Italy
1972—West Germany II

Four-Man

1924—Switzerland I
1928—United States II
1932—United States I
1936—Switzerland II
1948—United States II
1952—Germany
1956—Switzerland I
1960—Event not on program
1964—Canada I
1968—Italy I
1972—Switzerland I

*"I" indicates country's No. 1 team, "II" its No. 2 team.

BOBSLED (LUGE)
Single Seater—Men

1964—Thomas Koehler, Germany
1968—Manfred Schmid, Austria
1972—W. Scheidel, E. Germany

Two Seater—Men

1964—Austria

174

Gold Medal Winners Winter Olympics 1924–1972 / 175

1968—East Germany
1972—Italy

Single Seater—Women

1964—Otrum Enderlein, Germany
1968—Erica Lechner, Italy
1972—Anna Marie Muller, E. Germany

FIGURE SKATING
Men

1924—Gillis Grafstrom, Sweden
1928—Gillis Grafstrom, Sweden
1932—Karl Schafer, Austria
1936—Karl Schafer, Austria
1948—Richard Button, U.S.A.
1952—Richard Button, U.S.A.
1956—Hayes Alan Jenkins, U.S.A.
1960—David Jenkins, U.S.A.
1964—Manfred Schnelldorfer, Germany
1968—Wolfgang Schwarz, Austria
1972—Ondrej Nepela, Czech.

Women

1924—Herma Planck-Szabo, Austria
1928—Sonja Henie, Norway
1932—Sonja Henie, Norway
1936—Sonja Henie, Norway
1948—Barbara Scott, Canada
1952—Jeanette Altwegg, Gt. Britain
1956—Tenley Albright, U.S.A.
1960—Carol Heiss, U.S.A.
1964—Sjoukje Dijkstra, Netherlands
1968—Peggy Gale Fleming, U.S.A.
1972—Trixi Schuba, Austria

Pairs

1924—Helene Engelmann and Alfred Berger, Austria
1928—Andree Joly and Pierre Brunet, France
1932—Andree and Pierre Brunet, France
1936—Maxie Herber and Ernst Baier, Germany
1948—Micheline Lannoy and Pierre Baugniet, Belgium
1952—Ria and Paul Falk, Germany
1956—Elisabeth Schwarz and Kurt Oppelt, Austria
1960—Barbara Wagner and Robert Paul, Canada
1964—Ludmilla Beloussova and Oleg Protopopov, U.S.S.R.
1968—Beloussova and Protopopov, U.S.S.R.
1972—Irina Rodina and Alexei Ulanov, U.S.S.R.

ICE HOCKEY

1924—Canada
1928—Canada
1932—Canada
1936—Great Britain
1948—Canada
1952—Canada
1956—U.S.S.R.
1960—United States
1964—U.S.S.R.
1968—U.S.S.R.
1972—U.S.S.R.

SKIING
Alpine Events
MEN'S DOWNHILL

1948—Henri Oreiller, France
1952—Zeno Colo, Italy
1956—Anton Sailer, Austria
1960—Jean Vuarnet, France
1964—Egon Zimmermann, Austria
1968—Jean Claude Killy, France
1972—B. Russi, Switzerland

MEN'S SLALOM

1948—Edy Reinalter, Switzerland
1952—Othmar Schneider, Austria
1956—Anton Sailer, Austria
1960—Ernst Hinterseer, Austria
1964—Josef Stiegler, Austria
1968—Jean Claude Killy, France
1972—Francisco Ochoa, Spain

MEN'S GIANT SLALOM

1952—Stein Eriksen, Norway
1956—Anton Sailer, Austria
1960—Roger Staub, Switzerland
1964—Francois Boulieu, France
1968—Jean Claude Killy, France
1972—Gustav Thoeni, Italy

WOMEN'S DOWNHILL
1948—Hedy Schlunegger, Switzerland
1952—Gertrud Jochum-Beiser, Austria
1956—Madeline Berthod, Switzerland
1960—Heidi Biebl, Germany
1964—Christl Haas, Austria
1968—Olga Pall, Austria
1972—Marie Nadig, Switzerland

WOMEN'S SLALOM
1948—Gretchen Frazer, U.S.A.
1952—Andrea Mead Lawrence, U.S.A.
1956—Renee Colliaid, Switzerland
1960—Anne Haggtveit, Canada
1964—Christine Goitschel, France
1968—Marielle Goitschel, France
1972—Barbara Cochran, U.S.A.

WOMEN'S GIANT SLALOM
1952—Andrea Mead Lawrence, U.S.A.
1956—Ossi Reichert, Germany
1960—Yvonne Ruegg, Switzerland
1964—Marielle Goitschel, France
1968—Nancy Greene, Canada
1972—Marie Nadig, Switzerland

Nordic Events
MEN'S COMBINED
(15-KILOMETER CROSS COUNTRY AND JUMPING)
1924—Thorleif Haug, Norway
1928—Johan Grottumsbraaten, Norway
1932—Johan Grottumsbraaten, Norway
1936—Oddbjorn Hagen, Norway
1948—Heikki Hasu, Finland
1952—Simon Slattvik, Norway
1956—Sverre Stenersen, Norway
1960—Georg Thoma, Germany
1964—Tormond Knutsen, Norway
1968—Franz Keller, West Germany
1972—Ulrich Wehling, E. Germany

MEN'S 15-KILOMETER CROSS COUNTRY
1924—Thorleif Haug, Norway
1928—Johan Grottumsbraaten, Norway

1932—Sven Utterstrom, Sweden
1936—Erik-August Larsson, Sweden
1948—Martin Lundstrom, Sweden
1952—Hallgein Brenden, Norway
1956—Hallgein Brenden, Norway
1960—Haakon Brusveen, Norway
1964—Eero Maentyranta, Finland
1968—Harald Groenningen, Norway
1972—Sven Lundback, Sweden

MEN'S 30-KILOMETER CROSS COUNTRY
1956—Veikko Hakulinen, Finland
1960—Sixten Jernberg, Sweden
1964—Eero Maentyranta, Finland
1968—Franco Nones, Italy
1972—V. Vedenin, U.S.S.R.

MEN'S 50-KILOMETER CROSS COUNTRY
1924—Thorlief Haug, Norway
1928—Per Erik Hedlund, Sweden
1932—Veli Saarinen, Finland
1936—Elis Viklund, Sweden
1948—Nils Karlsson, Sweden
1952—Veikko Hakulinen, Finland
1956—Sixten Jernberg, Sweden
1960—Kalevi Hamalainen, Finland
1964—Sixten Jernberg, Sweden
1968—Ole Ellefsaeter, Norway
1972—Paal Tyldum, Norway

MEN'S SKI JUMPING (70 METERS)
1964—Veikko Kankkonen, Finland
1968—Jiri Raska, Czechoslovakia
1972—Yukio Kasaya, Japan

MEN'S SKI JUMPING (90 METERS)
1968—Vladimir Beloussov, U.S.S.R.
1972—W. Fortuna, Poland

MEN'S 4 × 10-KILOMETER RELAY
1936—Finland
1948—Sweden
1952—Finland

Gold Medal Winners Winter Olympics 1924–1972 / 177

1956—U.S.S.R.
1960—Finland
1964—Sweden
1968—Norway
1972—U.S.S.R.

WOMEN'S 5-KILOMETER CROSS COUNTRY

1964—Klaudia Boyarskikh, U.S.S.R.
1968—Toni Gustafsson, Sweden
1972—G. Kulakova, U.S.S.R.

WOMEN'S 10-KILOMETER CROSS COUNTRY

1952—Lydia Wideman, Finland
1956—Lyubov Kozireva, U.S.S.R.
1960—Maria Gusakova, U.S.S.R.
1964—Klaudia Boyarskikh, U.S.S.R.
1968—Toni Gustafsson, Sweden
1972—G. Kulakova, U.S.S.R.

WOMEN'S 3 × 5-KILOMETER RELAY

1956—Finland
1960—Sweden
1964—U.S.S.R.
1968—Norway
1972—U.S.S.R.

SPEED SKATING
Men's 500 Meters

	Sec.
1924—Charles Jewtraw, U.S.A.	:44.0
1928—Clas Thunberg, Finland and Bernt Everrsen, Norway	:43.4
1932—John Shea, U.S.A.	:43.4
1936—Ivar Ballangrud, Norway	:43.4
1948—Finn Helgesen, Norway	:43.1
1952—Ken Henry, U.S.A.	:43.2
1956—Yevgeni Grishin, U.S.S.R.	:40.2
1960—Yevgeni Grishin, U.S.S.R.	:40.2
1964—Terry McDermott, U.S.A.	:40.1
1968—Erhard Keller, W. Germany	:40.3
1972—Erhard Keller, W. Germany	:39.4

Men's 1,500 Meters

	Min.-Sec.
1924—Clas Thunberg, Finland	2:20.8
1928—Clas Thunberg, Finland	2:21.0
1932—John Shea, U.S.A.	2:57.5
1936—Charles Mathisen, Norway	2:19.2
1948—Sverre Farstad, Norway	2:17.6
1952—Hjalmar Andersen, Norway	2:20.4
1956—Yevgeni Grishin and Yuri Mikhailov, U.S.S.R.	2:08.6
1960—Yevgeni Grishin, U.S.S.R., and Roald Aas, Norway	2:10.4
1964—Ants Antson, U.S.S.R.	2:10.3
1968—Cornelius Verkerk, Netherlands	2:03.4
1972—Ard Schenk, Netherlands	2:03.0

Men's 5,000 Meters

	Min.-Sec.
1924—Clas Thunberg, Finland	8:39.0
1928—Ivar Ballangrud, Norway	8:50.5
1932—Irving Jaffee, U.S.A.	9:40.8
1936—Ivar Ballangrud, Norway	8:19.6
1948—Reidar Liaklev, Norway	8:29.4
1952—Hjalmar Andersen, Norway	8:10.6
1956—Boris Shilkov, U.S.S.R.	7:48.7
1960—Viktor Kositschkin, U.S.S.R.	7:51.3
1964—Knut Johannessen, Norway	7:38.4
1968—F. Anton Maier, Norway	7:22.4
1972—Ard Schenk, Netherlands	7:23.6

Men's 10,000 Meters

	Min.-Sec.
1924—Julius Skutnabb, Finland	18:04.8
1928—Event not held, due to thawing	
1932—Irving Jaffee, U.S.A.	19:13.6
1936—Ivar Ballangrud, Norway	17:24.3
1948—Ake Seyffarth, Sweden	17:26.3
1952—Hjalmar Andersen, Norway	16:45.8
1956—Sigvard Ericsson, Sweden	16:35.9
1960—Knut Johannesen, Norway	15:46.6
1964—Jonny Nilsson, Sweden	15:50.1
1968—Jonny Hoeglin, Sweden	15:23.6
1972—Ard Schenk, Netherlands	15:01.4

Women's 500 Meters

	Sec.
1960—Helga Haase, Germany	:45.9
1964—Lydia Skoblikova, U.S.S.R.	:45.0
1968—Lydmila Titova, U.S.S.R.	:46.1
1972—Anne Henning, U.S.A.	:43.3

Women's 1,000 Meters

	Min.-Sec.
1960—Klara Guseva, U.S.S.R.	1:34.1
1964—Lydia Skoblikova, U.S.S.R.	1:33.2
1968—Carolina Geijssen, Netherlands	1:32.6
1972—Monika Pflug, W. Germany	1:31.4

Women's 1,500 Meters

	Min.-Sec.
1960—Lydia Skoblikova, U.S.S.R.	2:25.2
1964—Lydia Skoblikova, U.S.S.R.	2:22.6
1968—Kaija Mustonen, Finland	2:22.4
1972—Dianne Holum, U.S.A.	2:20.9

Women's 3,000 Meters

	Min.-Sec.
1960—Lydia Skoblikova, U.S.S.R.	5:04.3
1964—Lydia Skoblikova, U.S.S.R.	5:14.9
1968—Johanna Schut, Netherlands	4:56.2
1972—S. Baas-Kaiser, Netherlands	4:52.1